AF263979

THE KEY TO A LONG LASTING MARRIAGE

The Ultimate Guidebook to Successfully Rekindling and Improving Your Marriage by Yourself, Without Unnecessarily Paying for Marriage Therapy

Written by Barnard W. Bunton

Table of Contents

Chapter 1: Introduction

Everyone has a dream of finding their soul mate. Men dream about that Princess, who lost her glass slipper, and they need to find her by visiting every house in the valley until a beautiful young lady fits into the slipper. Women dream about their Prince charming who comes to rescue them from the dragon and carries them off into the golden sunset. A handsome knight in shining armor, to be exact. Everyone has a fairytale. Everybody was longing for that love story that would last forever; each one of us has our own chosen story that we want to last a lifetime. What is your fairytale? Unfortunately, real-life does not have these types of fantasy fairytales, but that does not mean you cannot have one. In real life, we must adjust our sail to get to our destination.

The biggest fear that gives men and women a sense of insecurity towards Marriage is the big *"D."* That's right! Many people fear divorce. It does not matter if you have been married for three months or 30 years. Marriage is a big commitment and a huge decision. That is why I created this guide. In a sense, we can call it the ultimate guidebook for married couples.

We are going to reveal some secrets to improve or rekindle your Marriage. These secrets have been around for years, and you already probably know about many of them; while, others you may not have tried before.

Imagine you are a kid again. You are playing with Legos. These are the building blocks of creativity. These are the pieces that you want to design together. I am going to introduce some new building blocks. They will be the building blocks of Trust in Marriage.

Regardless of the type of Marriage you have, everyone needs some form of marriage counseling. I have created a guidebook that will help you through it. With the right motivation and determination, you do not need to pay the high cost of marriage counseling and therapies. It is time to transform your Marriage into something amazing. Everyone deserves to have a fairytale ending.

Be a Better Version of You Through a Marriage Transformation

What is marriage? Let us first define the word *"marriage"* before we begin talking about the different stages of married life.

Marriage Defined

Marriage is part of our history. It traces back to an ancient civilization, where the goal was to have a marriage act as an alliance between families. There was a system of rules to handle the granting of property rights and protection of bloodlines. In early history, marriage was not a relationship between a man and a woman like we know it today. It was mainly an obligation, to look after the property, and to maintain power among people involved.

Marriage is also an arranged alliance to strengthen and preserve morals and civilization. Usually, the head of the family decides to have his daughter arrange to marry for an economic reason; yet, not for courtship between two parties. The head of the family chooses somebody who can give full stability to his daughter. This arrangement has been historically prominent in many cultures and even being practiced in recent times. Throughout history, the value and meaning of marriage have differed in every view of a country, generation of people, religions, or traditions.

Marriage in recent times is somehow different from the past. Today, people decide to get married because they have been in a relationship for so long that it seems to be the next step to take. They feel they have found the one who will make them happy. They are ready to make that commitment to their soul mate that will give them a fairytale ending. They marry out of romance and courtship. They marry because they want to level up their dating relationship and want to secure through marriage whoever they desire to spend the rest of their lives. Today, marriage means so much more to this generation. It is no longer about the union of families for status and power. It is about a deeper understanding of your partner through the bonds of love, respect, more profound commitment, and trust.

Marriage, for some, is becoming a social status, and a wedding ceremony is turning into a symbol of someone's capacity to live. Most people marry during their adult lives, wherein ages were ranging from the twenties to thirties. During this time, most people experience the top of their careers, giving them a financial reason to make it more feasible and possible to carry out their obligations. It applies mainly to men because of their financial capability; to be wed determines his capacity to support a family, builds a house of their own, and be responsibly independent. Also, the underlying factors of marriage had changed after decades of generation.

Divorces and annulments have created a legal separation for the failed marriage. Divorces and annulments, for some, is an easy way out if you want out of the relationship. They are also for people who just got tired of being with that person. Throughout history, the definition of marriage is known by every age.

Marriage today is viewed as matrimony or wedlock, which is a communion of two people to live together bounded by love and underlying aspects of their relationship called husband and wife. They give each other legal rights and personal obligations of the union of two persons as partners in a personal connection. ***Marriage is personal. Marriage is an intimate companionship.***

A wedding is filled with aspects considered as unique, exclusive, intimate, and makes up the characteristics of an individual. It is always about the two people deciding to marry each other. It involves personal feelings to be able to choose who and why to marry. Like our growth from infancy to old age, we go through stages and personal development.

Marriage is personal development, and the event is a process that creates growth and change in terms of physical and emotional features. We age through time and stumble through valuable learnings along the way. We go through life with given a personal strength and perseverance.

Marriage is a valuable union. Through the next several pages, you will find relevant information to transform your Marriage. Start showing your spouse and family how much you love them. Marriage is essential, so make it last and make memories out of it. Being married is fun and exciting, so enjoy the taste and thrill of it.

Chapter 2: Stages of Marriage

As we go through this chapter, we will emphasize the word **_"personal,"_** as this will embody our point being made and makes up the entire content of the section. We will also highlight the stages married people experience through their personal growth. We will tackle each stage of marriage with situational examples applicable to most readers. You will be able to understand each step differently and associate it with your relationship.

Stage 1: The Romance Stage

Some call the first stage of marriage, the Romance or Honeymoon Stage, where romance and passion are the most intense and is the focus of the relationship. **_You are in a state of euphoria_** that makes you feel enthusiastic where you can see rainbows on a gloomy day. These emotions are powerful and significant. This stage usually happens a few months after the wedding. As you go through this stage, you feel magic in the morning. You can tell that every day is a beautiful day waking up next to the person you love. You want to cherish and savor every moment beside the person you love. You want to stop time and preserve every moment and forever. They are everything to you. You cannot live without them.

Significantly, you show the world how you both are in love with each other through social media, your network of friends, and a series of situations. You let your significant other know how much you value them verbally and physically. You are always on top of each other and discovering each personality. You are both proud and excited to take this journey together more than anything else. You desire your partner more now than you did during your courtship stage.

You view your marriage as the best decision you ever made in life. You are proud of your spouse. You want to climb to the highest mountain and shout it to the world that they are the perfect person for you. You listen to each other. You are willing to accept them through whatever flaws they have. You do what is necessary to satisfy your spouse and can keep your relationship going. You are most excited about your spouse and lonely whenever your partner is not around. You have patience and tolerance for this person because you always think having patience is the right thing to do. You approach things most sweetly. Everything is walking in the clouds at this stage.

When my wife and I first got married, I felt this same way. I wanted to climb the highest mountain and shout to the world, _"I found the girl of my dreams."_ It was such an exciting time. It was hard when we were apart. Even if those separations came because of work, granted, it was only an eight-hour shift. It was still hard to be alone. I want to rush through every minute of my every day in the workplace just to be with her. One hour was too long to be away from each other. The little things you do for each other will make a big difference. The short time you have with each other is full of magic. She is my fairytale.

You always show your best behavior to your spouse. You wanted to be the perfect match for your spouse. You do not want to commit any mistakes because it seems it's an A- to your points. You are a superhero in their eyes. You please your spouse in almost everything; wives are becoming domesticated, wherein they start learning different recipes to cook, how to improve the cleaning, organizing, and dressing differently from what they were before. They developed skills that only married people know, and they start behaving differently from when they were single. They are more responsible, reliable, and organized.

On the other note, husbands become more different too. They learn to make decisions together with their spouse. They start becoming dependent on their wives while sharing in every responsibility of their marriage, even taking turns washing the dishes. They see their relationship as an achievement, on how they have matured over time, and making such a big step. The men are the head of the family. They think that they are more mature and want their wives to rely on them as their partner. They take on the responsibility of supporting a family, providing all kinds of support, and building a home they can be proud of calling theirs. They give up their freedom and personal time to always be with their partner as the head of the family. They change their ways in life from being carefree and independent most of the time to becoming a caring and understanding husband and a responsible father.

Avoiding conflict is also ideal during this stage, and maintaining a harmonious relationship is a priority. Generally, both husbands and wives display good behaviors among each other. Negative emotions suppress to avoid marital problems. Strengthen the self-worth of your spouse by uncovering what pleases your spouse.

Building a foundation of marriage is essential during this stage, and avoiding conflict contributes to a peaceful relationship. Growing your relationship is a significant task, and personal development is a way to achieve your goals. This stage produces happy memories for the marital journey. This period usually lasts from two months to two years. It serves as a starting point to build a happy life with your partner.

Stage 2: The Disillusionment Stage

The Disillusionment Stage is also known as Awakening, Familiarization, or Adjusting to Reality Stage. Those delightful feelings brought about the romance stage is slowly fading away, and reality is starting to kick in. The truth is, both of you are humans; emotional, flawed, make mistakes, and have different personalities that you both commit errors and react in every situation, especially if it's not in favor of you personally. You wonder why your spouse is not the same person. Your eyes are starting to open, and you wonder why they are not more like you. At some point, these little differences start to annoy both of you. You feel bothered by some of the things you used to admire in your partner just a short time earlier and start questioning yourself if you had made the right choice.

You are starting to realize that the person you marry is far from perfect. You begin to understand that your spouse is not the person that you visualized him or her to be. You know that the good things brought about by the romance stage were somehow a fantasy that did not last long. You come to the point that consistency is off the menu, the giving of flowers, the courtship, walking in the clouds was an imaginary road. The staying at home most of the time, and the actions of love are slowly fading away.

Conflict often arises as a result of your indifferences, and negative emotions come pouring out. Irritations and little patience are starting to grow in this stage. Misunderstandings usually come in the way of achieving your goal. Communication is becoming a strain for both partners. Sometimes given by the perfect image painted by your romance stage, the disillusionment stage causes you to hurt and make you feel depressed. Expecting things that will never happen will feel cause annoyance. The person you thought that was heaven sent is giving you a headache.

This stage starts to challenge your relationship with each other. How your reactions impact the relationship and resolving a conflict depends on how deep your affection is towards each other. The value of your relationship shows at this stage. For some couples, this realization is too heart wrenching that they end their marriage during this stage. However, to overcome this, we must understand each situation as conflict arises due to personal indifference. Each spouse should consider knowing the motive of their action.

You must decide to love your spouse through thick and thin. Tell yourself marriage is not going to be a bed of roses. Somewhere along the way, there are thorns that you need to endure. Do not let your frustrations control you and make you regret it in the end. Stay right to your heart. Focus on the problems that arise. Do not say things that will make the problems worse; instead, offer encouragement and solutions. Give your partner space to breathe when things get rough. Suggest small footsteps in coming up with the answers. Let them know you are there for them by their side. Tell them that you will stick together for better and when things get worse.

Communication between partners is a key to resolving conflicts and is a skill you learn if you want your relationship to continue. Communicating will help you to improve your ability to listen to your partner. Communication is understanding the needs of your partner and can level things between both of you. Marriage is personal; therefore, to get the better of this stage, you must make each decision to resolve every personal conflict. You must be willing to do anything to settle all the negative interactions and emotions that will weigh your relationship down. Make all your actions private and about the two of you. The choice of words we use is the reflection of how much we are trying so hard to communicate. The choices you make as a couple to resolve conflicts will pave the way to a successful journey of life.

Understanding and accepting all the flaws of your significant other could come a long way; after all, marriage is about acknowledging everything this beautiful journey has to offer. Marriage is a two-way action; do something, and you will get something.

Stage 3: The Power Struggle Stage

Why do you experience these power struggles? It is easier to play the "blame game." The battle comes from sharing your needs and feeling with your partner. That is why this stage is more commonly known as the Disappointment or Distress Stage. Conflicts always get worse when couples find themselves in a power struggle. You feel you are not satisfied in the relationship due to your needs not being fulfilled. Each spouse digs in more. You may find yourself attacking the character of your spouse because you think your spouse never understands your pain. At worst, disagreement gets so big, and you develop hatred, which is unhealthy in the relationship.

Most couples do not get past this stage and find themselves considering a marriage separation or divorce is the only solution they can find. Thinking that they do not need to deal with their spouse anymore comes into play. The overall emotion carried out by the disillusionment stage becomes intense and hard to solve. It puts your marriage into a critical phase. Conflict becomes hard enough to deal with, and you may find your relationship struggling, and the troubles get worse. Communicating to hear each other's side is nonexistent. Couples are more into getting mad and irritated.

Often, during this stage, marriage starts to deteriorate slowly, and the vows and promises once made begin to drifting away. These are the times' couples seek the counsel of a family, friend, or marriage counselor to resolve disputes. You feel your spouse does not see your point of view. You think that you are the greatest enemy of your partner who will prosecute you. They are having a hard time compromising on a solution because, in the first place, they don't want to listen to you anymore. They are stubborn and insist on always taking the lead in all the decisions. At times, your spouse thinks they are right, and you are wrong, and proving you wrong makes them feel they are right. You both feel your way is the best way to handle the situation, and their approach will not work as well. You may begin to work things out with your partner; yet, it makes the situation worse. You will start to pull away from each other to have a clear mind and ease the tension between the two of you.

The power struggle stage in marriage is both stable and rewarding. As a couple, you both need to understand what this stage is and what sets it off when it happens.

Those simple annoyances from stage two have become clear to you that you probably have chosen the wrong partner in life. You often fight even over small things, and you don't seem to settle it the way you like. You may start viewing your partner as a person sent by God to make your life difficult. You begin to think of them as self-center, egocentric, immature, uncaring, or a person that cannot be trusted and needs to dump in the curb. You wonder if you ever encounter the type of personality your spouse had before getting married. You feel like you forced yourself into marrying them, which makes it worse.

Marital affairs occur more during this stage, as couples start to drift apart from each other. They tend to look for attention that they do not get from their partner. They form sexual relationships, romantic relationships, or create a passionate attachment to other people without their partner knowing; hence, they go back to stage one where happiness and excitement overrules.

At some point, things start to deteriorate in the relationship, and you fight more, and getting mad is just the usual thing. Finding more faults towards your spouse just to argue becomes a habit. Sexual intimacy no longer exists; no excitement for sex and making love is merely an obligation than a passion for privacy; it feels more like a release of tension than deeply felt love. Personal affection is slipping away, and every so often, we find this hole filled by other people through a marital affair. You tend to forget that you are bound by being married to your spouse, and you develop new feelings for others.

Many relationships fail when they feel their spouse does not care about their needs. You go your separate ways and eventually fall in love as you begin stages one through three, making the cycle repeat itself. Between an ineffective conflict resolution style and the growing pressure of life, couples may start to doubt their compatibilities during this stage. However, conquering this stage will be gratifying in the end. The disillusionment stage does not prove that you are with the wrong partner but instead challenges you personally to fix any disagreements that come in your relationship.

It takes a lot of willingness, persistence, and continuous forgiveness to make your relationship better. There is a constant cycle of understanding the person you chose to marry. With effective communication and constructive conflict resolution, you can work together through your problems and find better solutions. Ultimately, the couple who fight for their marriage to become better are the marriages that are worth fighting to keep.

You could be in this stage for several years. They say that if your marriage lasts past eight years of marriage, you already overcome the trials and hardship. You were up to the challenge that you have chosen the right person no matter what, and you are willing to stick by their side in through the good or bad. Most separations and divorces happen before the eight-year mark of marriage. However, there are a small few that occur after eight years.

Stage 4: The Stability Stage

The Stability Stage is also known as the Friendship or Reconciliation Stage. The relationship becomes acceptable with each partner, and you both set limitations to the things that you want. There are freedoms and your own choices at this stage. The storm is gone, and you enter the stage where you start to feel the calm. Some couples did not make it through the rain to see this stage, but those who make it to this stage learn some valuable lessons about each other.

Accepting your partner's flaws is a vital part of any relationship, and taking the personal decision to forgive no matter how hurt you are. It is rewarding when your partner meets your feelings, and you accept the fact that your partner is not perfect. You start to take the way your spouse feels, beliefs, opinions, and flaws. It is not your job to change who they are; instead, be a guide to them, accept them for who they are and what they become by helping them become a better person and spouse.

Reconciliation after every conflict will become essential. You learn to discuss the causes and effects of your disagreement. You are learning to go back from the purpose of the issue, making it easier to create solutions to avoid the problem from happening the next time. You start sharing your thoughts and feelings more with your partner. Both of you learn to check each other's points of view. You consider what your partner wants and needs in your relationship as you move forward. You begin to start realizing there are more things that you can do in your relationship. You take your time to tackle what you want from your connection to continue this great journey. You decide to walk side by side, hand in hand for the one path you both are aiming for in this great union.

During this time, those things that puzzled you before have become more evident; for starters, you don't get mad anymore if he bought some expensive tools for a hobby. You are starting to realize that it is only petty things that get on your nerves, and it is not even worth the arguments. You now start understanding this is his way to ease some tension at work and his outlet during stressful times. You did not get upset if she buys a pair of new shoes even though she already has 50 pairs that do not get worn; instead, you just think that maybe she just wants a variety of designs with those shoes. You know she likes shoes, and there may be a time where she needs them for a new outfit.

You are now putting yourself into each other's situations. You also start learning that your spouse may get grumpy all the time because they are exhausted and having a bad day, and it will only take you to watch over chores, babysitting the kids, and let them have a rest. Eventually, they will be okay with your help in doing their daily tasks. In other words, you start looking at your spouse with the eyes of seeing what was there when you were dating. You begin to see who they are and begin to remember why you love them in the first place. You start seeing the things that you both were doing for each other when you were still dating, and eventually, the magical moments will come back!

As you enter this stage, you deeply put the word *"personal"* into your marriage. You are consistently learning that you and your partner are different. Even twins have a different perspective on life. You accept your partner is not perfect because as you live together each day, mistakes are like routine, people will commit mistakes even how much they try not to. The good thing is we learn something from our mistakes. You started to grasp the reality that marriage is not a walk in the park holding a dozen balloons.

Instead of giving up, you both find solutions and learn the tools on how to keep your marriage alive. Do things that you never did when you were still dating. Discover new hobbies or sports that you and your spouse will love. Go and plan for a short vacation. Go for a long drive at night to get some fresh air. These are some of the ways that you can also add to your relationship. Be creative, and at the same time, you are learning with your partner. You learn that there are individual attainable skills, attitudes, and means you both can deal with unavoidable problems your relationship will encounter. You and your partner value the word *"compromise"* most of all. You start to synchronize and resolve each conflict in a better way that provides support in the relationship.

Connect your needs and wants to your partner so you will begin to realize what makes you both happy and satisfied. You both take steps together, making sure no one is left behind. Taking those steps together, you and your spouse feel that everything will be okay. Whatever trials that arise again, you are both aware that you can fight back together. You begin to achieve the goals you have set in the first place, and wanting to materialize those plans is an excellent feeling. In marriage, all we want is a happy and satisfying life, and everything will follow.

The battle is not over yet since this is a never-ending process. To make your marriage last longer, you need to fill up your strength and keep going. Make sure you keep filling those marriage cups that you both are holding. Fill those cups with love, commitment, and want to be by each other's side. It will have been regretful and waste if your marriage deteriorates at this stage. After all, you worked hard to reach this stage. You fought back all those odds and stain that tried to ruin your relationship. You need to find the reason why and how you made it from step two and ended up in step four. Continue with the push and courage to continue in the process. Endure what is hard and telling yourself, I can do this. Remember, there is a rainbow after the rain. Make everything personal and focus on what you feel inside. Remember the things you could have lost if you will give up the fight. Recollect those sweet moments that you and your spouse promised to love each other until gray hairs. Thinking about those past good memories is a big help in reconnecting because sometimes what the mind forgets, the heart remembers.

You and your spouse should be the best of friends, confidantes, and supporters. My wife and I have been through a lot. We have had our differences and arguments. However, we are best friends and partners. We do not have many friends; although, the ones we do have are couples. We do everything together. Even after all these years, it does not feel right to go anywhere if we are not together. If friends invite us to go somewhere, the first person we think of is each other. We do not go with friends if we are not together. I enjoy this aspect of our marriage. There is no one I would rather spend time with than my wife.

As you move onto the next stage, you will find that you will always be in the friendship stage; only, it has changed to a higher level.

Stage 5: The Commitment Stage

The Commitment Stage can also be considered the Love Phase, Acceptance, or Transformation Stage. This phase is where you know all the worse cases that could happen in a relationship; yet, you still chose to stay together. You realized there is no perfect spouse in the world nor an ideal relationship, but that does not matter as you decide to stay together. In this stage, you know that you love your spouse, but sometimes they are not the best of a person. They are the cause of your headache and irritation, but still, you decided to settle down with this person as it is the best choice you have made in life. You no longer imagine life without your chosen mate, which means the level of resentment you felt after undergoing each stage has somehow decreased. You both consciously love each other through thick and thin. Making your love the center of your relationship through a deep love that you know and understand that you like each other.

Due to the experiences and what you learn from stage four, you have started to apply your "lessons learned" whenever a situation turns sour. The value of *"compromise"* and working together has become an essential aspect of your marriage. You start recognizing married life can be beautiful after all, and marital recognition is alluring.

You learned how to genuinely love your partner more than the first time you met them. Start to experience the balance of power, freedom, and belongingness. You put their priorities before your own. When two people can put aside their differences to reignite the love they once shared, everybody wins. It was not always easy, but it sure was worth trying. Reality has set in, and you can see that you are both humans. You make mistakes in your relationship. However, you learn to appreciate each other by enjoying the company of your partner. You pick your partner above anybody else.

This stage can consider you as triumphant; you are now joining the league of successful marriages. Couples finally realize that a successful marriage does not happen in a day, and it is never all sweetness and light. There is nothing better in the world than living your lives together, learning to love deeply, selflessly, and passionately. You realize that you only have each other, so focus intently on the essential building blocks of a healthy and fruitful marriage.

Through all those stages, it is necessary to consider the factors that contribute to a happy and healthy marriage. First and foremost, love is the main point of a relationship. Loving your spouse is the driving force for you to keep going despite the problems. Love gives meaning to all you do for your partner, no matter if it is small or big to make a marriage work. Loving your spouse makes you forget all the wrong sides in the relationship.

Love and marriage go together like a carriage to a horse. With this vital commitment, love is a decision made to another person that you will always be by their side, helping and nourishing them. Those times that make you feel like quitting will help you to remember your commitment. The old times that you made a promise to them that you will always be around whatever happens. You have given your word to your partner during this union that you will be as one *"till death do us part."* It takes dedication and love to stay with one person, building a lifetime of respect for your spouse, and keep going through the ups and downs.

Next is sexual faithfulness. Tell yourself that you are not single and already taken. It is not common for a married man to come looking for attention from others when he does not get enough from his spouse. Sexual faithfulness involves not just your body but also your eyes, mind, heart, and soul. Refuse to put anything in front of your eyes, body, and thoughts. Do not let it compromise your faithfulness to your partner. Always guard your sexual intimacy. Stay away from the things that could get your interest aside from your spouse. If you know someone who tried to get your attention, do not be fascinated, and show no excitement. Tell that person that you are not interested and simply walk away. Avoid that person and have an escape plan the next time around is also a big help. Do not think of yourself being with someone else; what matters is you are in a relationship, and you already commit yourself to your marriage and your spouse.

Next is patience and forgiveness, which goes hand and hand to make your relationship work and last a lifetime. Make everything personal about your partner. In times of mistakes, you let patience and forgiveness rule. Do not seek revenge to make amends when your partner commits errors, and most of all, do not bring in past mistakes to get even. Think to yourself that one day, you might need forgiveness from your spouse too. One day the situations might get reversed, and you are the one who wants understanding and forgiveness. Having to forgive someone who hurt you is a decision you make and not what you feel. Forgiveness is a need for success in your relationship.

All the stages of your union will make you an effective communicator where you value communication more as critical when producing resolutions. Also, communication is about relaying not only on essential things with your partner but on emotional needs such as interests, passions, dreams, and anxieties. You harness your ability to communicate more effectively.

Finally, in some cases, your relationships are broken up because of selfishness than any other reason. People tend to do things that only benefit one person and will result in a misunderstanding between the married couple. Given all the stages that I have discussed, it shows that when you are married, you give up your self-interest to prioritize the well-being of your spouse and your family. Thinking about how your spouse will react before making a decision will somehow affect the whole household. You become selfless in your choice, knowing that your family matters the most.

There is no formula for success when it comes to a relationship, just communicate openly to your spouse and be honest about everything. Nobody had done it better than anybody else. All couples have gone through the same thing but at different times and different levels of misunderstanding. Each one has its time frame, but everybody still needs the same ingredients to master the recipe for an excellent bond for a lasting marriage. It takes a lot of perseverance and determination to make it work. There are many areas of closeness that enhances the strength of a relationship for it to remain healthy and help get it back unstuck once it stumbles.

Mastering each key to a successful union is not easy; you might give up along the way, or you keep fighting but, it can help the connection thrive. The keys can maintain a relationship to become more satisfying and closer to make it worth challenging.

To maintain a happy relationship with your partner is not an easy task; yet, as you go through each stage, you start to realize conflicts are smaller than your determination to pursue happiness. Knowing that fights and arguments are expected for any relationship, you will begin to understand that you are lucky enough to know these things and gets a solution. There is no argument too big that we cannot forgive and forget, and no relationship is higher than the ones you went through in battle to make it last. If you don't take marriage by heart, it will slowly dissolve and deteriorate and will be slowly drifting away. If you decide to fight for your relationship, it can become a great achievement and a great battle that we have to surpass. Having a great relationship is knowing you can rely on each other and can function independently of each other. To have a good relationship, you need to have trust and allow the other person to be themselves, giving them the freedom to express their needs and wants while committing and loving them unconditionally.

Chapter 3: A Deeper Understanding of Marriage

Part of a great relationship is to understand each other by knowing yourself, start trusting, be a good listener, and always forgive. Marriage takes work, dedication, respect, and love. Unfortunately, this does not happen overnight. It takes time to develop this understanding. Both partners must do their part, and it is not a one-person show. Communicate often by sharing what you are thinking and your feeling. They say the first seven years of a marriage are the most critical, where lots of things could have to happen if you are not strong enough to hold on. If you strengthen your Marriage during those years, you will last a lifetime in each other's arms. Adding humor and combine with the magic of small things are vital ingredients for a new marriage. Partners should assist each other to grow in a useful way through a tender push or encouraging word. Accept your partner's passions and allowing them to explore. Learning your spouse's language of love is also essential.

Marriage Takes Work, Dedication, Respect, and Love.

Your relationship should begin to have a deeper connection. Over time, it will gradually develop. Most couples spend their entire Marriage getting to know each other and learning the do's and don't of each other. Just because you have this deeper connection does not mean you stop learning about your partner. It is essential to have a deeper understanding of your partner.

Acknowledge the feelings of your spouse even if you think they are minor or irrelevant. Be aware of your spouse's goal and resolution. Do not take them lightly, and you must be serious about how they feel. Give them a daily touch through a hug, kiss, or massage. Let them know how much they mean to you and how lucky you are by having them by your side. Express your gratitude you have for them. Say thank you and how much you appreciate the things they do. Listen to them continuously. They need to feel you have heard them because you know their needs better than anyone else. Instead of presuming what your spouse said, try asking for clarification of what you heard and give positive feedback. To understand what your partner feels is as important as what you are feeling.

One of the things that you need to put in your relationship is laughter, as sharing a good laugh makes for a healthy relationship. Laughter can lessen the tension when things get tough and help you get rid of the anxiety between you and your spouse. When boredom is starting to get in the way, laughter is the best tranquilizer. Having a good laugh can help you both cope with the pressures that surround your married life. Remember the times you both have shared in a good laugh. We can not develop feelings and attachments to anybody with whom we never laugh. Look around us and create a fun atmosphere with your partner. Share in the unforgettable memories and laugh at them. You can not continue getting mad at someone who makes you laugh. Some people say, *"laughter is an instant vacation from the negatives."* Do not forget to laugh at the jokes of your spouse. Being polite to your spouse is also needed, so go with the flow, relax, lighten up, and remember what matters in your marriage.

The needs of women and men have changed over time. It used to be the woman who stays home and takes care of the family while the man goes out and works to pay the bills. Some families still do this today. However, times have changed. The economy has changed, and people evolve. People have so much technology that even at home, you can get an online job. Women and men are born leaders, and they are now educated and smart. They go to university to further their education and getting a degree. Men are no longer the only breadwinner. Women also can help with family finances. They are equal and can do the jobs men can do. They know how to work together to get a stable income.

It is time to start understanding each other. Women are looking for someone who loves and appreciates them, not necessarily a perfect man, but a man who they can depend on in times of trouble. They want to feel accepted in a man's world. They long for a man who they can respect, look up to, and will stand by her side.

Women are true leaders, but sometimes they also get vulnerable at times. They need a man who can listen and can acknowledge their vulnerability.

Women will help you guide their relationship when they have a man who stands by her and provides support. A woman is the cornerstone of the family. They say that behind every great man is a woman who cares about the family.

Men long for a compassionate partner who is gentle and warm who share their beliefs and makes them a better man. A wife who is reliable, dependable, and has ambition in what he wants. They want a partner who supports and encourages them. Many men want a woman who knows what to do when things get hard. While other men wish to have someone who will bend down to their decision and never second guess the choices they make.

Men want an attractive companion, both on the inside and outside—a woman who can give suggestions and opinions. Men wish to have somebody who has a strong intuition and remembers every detail. Men want someone who can spend time with their family, friends, and cares about them as much as he does since marriage is a connection of two individuals existing before meeting each other.

You can start to see why it is so essential to understand your partner. Think about when you first started to date. What were you like? Did you share everything about your life? Most of us do not. It is not until you start falling in love with each other that you begin to let your partner know about your personal life. It is not until you are ready for that person to enter your innermost feeling that you begin to start trusting them.

One of the most important things you need to understand is the primary needs of men and women. Yes, we all have needs that are most important to each of us. These needs may vary from person to person; what you need in the relationship is not what most people want for theirs. They will not be the same for everyone. However, these will be a simple guide to help you start to understand the basic needs of each other. To fully understand the needs of your spouse, it requires communication.

Major Needs of Women

The primary needs of women will be slightly different from person to person. These are the most essential top five needs for women.

#1 – Affection: Women need to feel like they are loved and needed. Affection for a woman does not mean sex. It means showing a woman you love them through other ways. Try giving your wife flowers or sweet notes to show them you love them, and you remember them. Women need to feel beautiful every day by showing those simple gestures that make their hearts flutter.

Your wife needs to be number one. She needs to experience and feel she is the lady of your heart, making her more essential than your parents, children, friends, hobbies, and sports.

Share your affection with your wife by telling her how much you love her. Most women will never get tired of hearing those three simple words, *"I love you."* Actions always express louder than words. Your simple activities like an unexpected hug, holding hands, cuddling time during a movie, and a kiss are simple ways of showing your affection.

#2 – Conversation: Most women want to talk through their issues and day. Be an active listener and communicate with them. It is essential to open those lines of communication in the relationship.

Make your conversations with your wife meaningful. Do not only focus on the children, job, or weather. There is so much more to talk about beyond the typical everyday things. It is essential to discuss your thoughts and sentiments because those deep conversations are the glue that will hold your relationship together.

#3 – Honesty: One of the most important things to have in a relationship is honesty. Nobody wants someone lying to them. You should be an open book to your spouse and go both ways. Even if it is not on the top 5 for men, it is just as essential to be an open book with each other.

Most of the time, it is not easy to express our thoughts, wants, and needs to our significant other even when we want honesty. We are always bothered by the way they may react, so we think it is better to hold it inside. Hiding your sentiments will not do any good since we all need honesty in the relationship.

Honesty requires you to work together. It is giving and taking. If you expect honesty, then you must be honest in return. Remember, you are on the same team. When something happens with you or your partner, you should always have an open mind when the issues are talked about before either of you get mad or frustrated. Keep in mind, you and your spouse did not mean to cause hurt; maybe, it was unintentional or an accident.

There is a time and place for everything; which, includes honesty. An in-depth conversation requires honesty. Schedule the time you and your spouse can sit down and talk. Pay attention to their needs. Do not approach them with a situation that could make it worse. You should pick the right time to talk, such as during your afternoon walk, at dinner, before bed, or set time you both agree upon.

#4 – Financial Support: Every woman wants to be with a man who can provide financial support and has a business plan in place. You do not need to be wealthy. However, they want a man who can provide for their family.

Smart women are not only looking for the way a man looks or if they are a smooth talker; instead, they are looking at the way a man budgets and spends money. Does he spend his money outside of his budget, or does he set aside money into a savings account? A woman wants to be able to connect financially and not just on an intimate degree.

#5 – Family Commitments: Women have a secure family connection and want a man who has the same goals. A woman wants a mature man who does not go out clubbing with his buddies every night and searching for other women in public or online. They want a man who has an appreciation for their families and loved ones.

All of us need commitment. It gives us the security to show our partner they are safe, and you will do everything you can to support them because responsibility is a long-term goal.

The way a man treats their mother says a lot about the way they will treat their wives. Women are the backbone of the family unit. They have a secure connection to your children. While the men are making money to support the family financially, the women are taking care of the family.

Major Needs of Men

The primary needs of men will be slightly different from person to person. These are the basic top five needs for men. You will find that they are different from a woman's needs.

#1 – Intimacy: Intimacy entails the feelings of emotional closeness when connecting with another person. For many men, sex is a priority. However, intimacy is also more than sex. It can be doing things together as a couple. They feel making love is a way of showing their affection towards their spouse. Guys feel if their spouse will not make love to them regularly, then there is something wrong. Therefore, this is a basic need for a man to feel the love from their partner.

To build real intimacy with your man, you will do things together and make them feel the need you have for them. You can do simple things such as watching television, sex, sports, and hobbies together. The most important thing to take from this is it is about doing things as a couple.

Learn how each other communicates. Men and women communicate in different ways. Women communicate through how they feel, while men communicate through reality and facts.

#2 – Recreational Companionship: Basically, a recreational companion is someone who you do activities that involves doing things together. A lot of men enjoy the outdoors or being active. They seek a partner who enjoys the same things. They want someone to be there, do something with them, and make it one of their priorities, too. It should be something you both enjoy. Make this time as a golden opportunity to have pleasurable moments together. When men see that you are not excited about the activities, they do not feel passionate about it. If they are going to go hiking, do it as a family.

The time you spend as a couple is worth the effort, and your husband considers you as his favored recreational companion. Use this time to make memories together.

#3 – Attractive Spouse: Beauty is in the eye of the beholder. Men see their wives having an angelic face. Let's face it! Men want an attractive wife. They walk proud, and they want someone who other guys will look at and say, *"Man, he is one lucky guy."*

Guys also see the hearts of their women. Real beauty comes from inside. They take pride in the way they look. They like a woman who can carry a good conversation in public, always look beautiful, respect themselves, good personal hygiene, and care for the family.

#4 – Domestic Support: Domestic Support is also referred to as an Emotional Need for most men. They feel content when their wife meets these needs. Men want to have a well-managed environment at home. They want peace in the home and not chaos. This support is through washing the dishes, cooking meals, ironing the clothes, cleaning the house, and taking care of the children. Even as times have changed, this is still in the top 5 needs.

#5 – Admiration and Respect: Respect is accepting your spouse for who they are even when they do things differently, and you do not sympathize with them. Having respect in your relationship creates trust, protection, security, and wellbeing.

Like women, men want to feel like they are needed. They crave admiration and respect in the home. It is a two-way streak. One of the easiest ways to create chaos in the house is to show your partner disrespect.

Men feel love and respect when their wives spend time with them. For example, if he is into his game, you should cuddle next to him and watch the game together. It is not about the game. He just wants you to be closer. Also, saying you are sorry when you did something wrong is a way to show respect towards him.

Look at each of these lists. Do you see something different? Each one is different from the other. Men and women have different ways of looking at their affections and needs. Not everyone will have the same top five. That is why it is so essential to make your lists.

The key is to focus on the needs of your spouse. Do not show them the way you want it to be. Focus on the needs of your spouse. Women typically want affection outside of the bedroom. Men need to focus on the needs of their women. Men usually want to love inside the bedroom. Women should focus on the needs of their men. Granted, not all men and women are like this. Find ways to be intimate with your spouse on their level. This simple act will open your spouse up to an emotional connection.

Take the time to start writing your top five needs. You may have more than five. When this happens, combine needs that are alike until you have five. The next step is to share your lists with your spouse. That is the natural part. It is time to start focusing on each other's needs and not your own. Find ways that you can fulfill the needs of your spouse on their level.

Chapter 4: Marriage & Family Assessment

Assessing your Marriage is one of the most important things you can do. It helps to strengthen your relationship with each other. It does not matter if you have been married for six months or 30 years. It is essential to maintain an assessment of your Marriage and family.

I originally was going to focus only on Marriage. However, like most marriages, you start to have children. Children bring new light to your relationship and other challenges that affect your Marriage and children. Therefore, I will be adding a small part of the family connection in your relationship.

Marriage Assessment

When you are married, you make a vow or promise to each other. You commit to staying by each other's side and being together through all the good and bad times. You promise to support each other and be with your spouse, not wanting someone else. Every year, there are about 200,000 married couples who never make it to year two. That is a lot.

How you go through marriage depends on how you see things between you and your partner. An interpersonal relationship is about how you and your spouse connect on resolving differences so that no arguments will arise. It is also vital to know how you feel towards your partner, the thoughts you have in mind if you are upset, the things that bother you, and even unsettled discussions are essential.

Assessing the state of your relationship is essential because it is time you check how you make crucial decisions for the family as a couple, and if you will have a possible argument after deciding. One way to check who is the most sensitive is if your partner does not meet your needs.

In marriage, you do not need to stop getting to know each other through spending more quality time. Give your spouse the feeling that they are essential, and you need them. Focusing on the positive side is necessary, so when the time comes that your spouse commits mistakes, forgiving them is easy. Holding on to each other is a way of knowing you chose your spouse above anybody else, and you are willing to carry on whatever happened.

The goal is to strengthen your relationship with each other, so you will not be a statistic. The best place to start is through a marriage assessment. When thinking about your evaluation, I want you to focus on the areas that follow.

Teamwork: This is an essential part of a relationship. You should approach every situation together as a team. You are married. There is no longer "I" in the things you do. For example, if you want to buy an expensive purse or a new motorcycle, you must talk about it as this is not a decision to make as an individual. You should see it as a team decision. If you have a family, it is impossible without the other person. Approach every choice you make as a couple. Put in your mind that it is impossible to make this choice without talking to each other.

Teamwork talks about giving and not being self-centered in the relationship by being aware of your spouse's needs. Working as a team brings a closer connection to your partner while it builds and allows us to grow as a person and a group.

The goodness of a healthy and happy marriage has something big in stock, such as the same characteristic, opinions, and interests. A happy marriage does things together as one and creating a powerful team. Happy marriages are founded by teamwork, respect for each other's needs, and never-ending love.

Respecting your spouse is also treating them with kindness, patience, and tolerance. Being considerate and wanting to support one another. Cheering them up when they are sad and lonely tells you that you value them too.

A relationship is built on teamwork for you to always win. You and your spouse will never put the other down in any circumstances. Instead, you encourage and lift each other when there is a sign of weaknesses.

Maturity and Acceptance: As a couple, you are there for one another. You must accept who the other person is. This acceptance includes all the good and evil in who they are. You help each other to become more mature. You are the one who can bring your spouse to a higher level. It is because of you they are a better person.

For example, I have been writing for many years before I met my wife. I was living in fear and not sure if others would enjoy my writing. It has always been my passion. Through the encouragement from my spouse, I started to write and let others see my handwriting. Receiving feedback from my friends and family was encouraging. I could not have done it without my spouse being a part of my life. Through her encouragement and support, I can finally pursue my dream without being afraid of what others think.

Community and Faith: The most successful couples invite a spiritual presence into their lives. However, not everyone is religious. The choice should always be made together. Do you feel it is essential, or is it not relevant to you as a couple?

Many times, when a couple comes from two different religions and beliefs, it will cause chaos. This is a touchy subject. You form a union together and make the commitment to be with each other, which includes respecting the beliefs of each other.

When my wife and I started dating, we knew of our different beliefs. We were brought up differently. We begin to learn about each other's ideas. We respect each other and the way they think. When we started to have a family, we then had to decide as a couple on how we raise our family.

Just because we have our differences does not mean we cannot work together and respect each other. These beliefs are a part of who you are. What you believe in helps mold you into the person you show to your spouse.

Wealth-Building: As a couple, you should build your wealth. However, I leave a cation, do not allow it to be the center of your Marriage. When wealth becomes the center of the relationship, you are setting yourself up for failure. Having financial health is excellent. Although, is it more critical than your Marriage? The answer should be *"No."* All you have is each other.

When something terrible happens, and you lose that wealth, but your spouse will be by your side through the rough times. There is a saying, *"you cannot buy happiness."* Money should never be more important than the relationship you create with your spouse.

"You Cannot Buy Happiness."

A Healthy Lifestyle: Living a healthy lifestyle is essential. This includes getting enough sleep, eating healthily, and getting plenty of exercises. You will find yourself in a better mood and energized for the day. When we go to the gym, many times, we exercise with a workout partner. Why not have your spouse be your workout partner. It will give you a chance to bring your partnership even closer.

Motivate Each Other to be Healthier.

My wife and I use to take a trip to the gym regularly. There was nothing better than working out together. It gave us a chance to talk and motivate each other throughout our workouts. When finances got tight, we stopped going to the gym. It made a significant impact on the motivation to work out and stay healthy. What we did was start building our home gym. It is not much, but it does keep us healthy without needing to go out. We can still work out together and continue to motivate each other into a more active and better life as a couple.

Success in the Workplace: Supporting each other is essential. This is also true in the Workplace. Your Workplace could be at the office or at home. It does not matter if you work in fast food or as a homemaker. Perhaps you homeschool your children. Supporting each other is essential.

How do you support your spouse? There is a saying, *"behind every successful man is an amazing woman."* The saying is true because the backbone of many marriages is the wife, and they are the most supportive person in the relationship. However, the saying can also be the same when reversed. *"Behind every successful woman is an amazing man."*

Seeing that it takes support from each other, we could say, *"behind every successful marriage, there is a couple who supports each other."*

Behind Every Successful Marriage, There Is a Couple Who Supports Each Other.

Being a Good Neighbor: Each person brings their talents and gifts into the relationship. Use your skills and grants to support each other and be a good neighbor. Be there for your neighbors when you see them struggling. Do it as a couple.

Everyone has a neighbor. However, this does not only refer to your neighbors that live next door. For example, if you are going to the store and you see someone stranded on the side of the road. You know they are in trouble. You should be willing to stop and help them. Perhaps they are out of gas or having car troubles. Even if you do not know anything about cars, you can either give them a ride to a gas station, mechanic or call someone who can help them if you do not feel comfortable about giving them a ride.

Be an Outstanding Caregiver: Part of the promise you made to each other is to always be there through sickness and health. It is your job to take care of your spouse. If they are sick, you should take care of them until they are healthy again. If there is a family crisis, you are there for each other through the hard times. If it is a personal crisis, talking to each other and working through it together.

Many years ago, my wife ended up in the ICU at the hospital. She lost so much blood they put about four bags of blood back into her body before she was no longer in a critical state. I almost lost her. Just moments before, she died on the floor of a store just as the paramedics arrived. They revived her. During this time, I took the family and rushed to the hospital to be by her side. I still needed to provide for the family to make ends meet. Suddenly, I found myself juggling work, taking care of the children, and being by her side. It is a scary thing when you realize the love of your life is in that situation with the possibility of leaving us. Every day, I am grateful that she is still here by my side. It is those times where you need to care for each other.

Your Friendship Matters: Many couples think they need to find friends outside of the Marriage. Your spouse is your best friend. If you need friends outside of the relationship, you should make friends as a couple. This will give you protection from the temptations that I talk about later.

Your Spouse is Your Best Friend.

When my spouse and I were dating, we did everything together. It was like I found my best friend. During those times, I could not see her, and I would find a way to let her know she is missed. When I finally had time to stop by, I would stop and pick up some flowers. Even today, after being married for several years, we are still best friends and do everything together. It is not the same if you go out with other friends. Therefore, we usually go out alone and together. You must have a friendship that will last until the end of time.

Want Children Together: Children bring a new light into your Marriage. You will feel like you are not ready to have children. This feeling will never leave your mind. The truth is, having kids is a life-changing experience, and you are never fully prepared. It should be something you decide on together. After all, you cannot have children by yourself. You are a team, and they can only come into this world with the help of both of you.

The strength of your Marriage will determine the power of your family. Let your children see you as a team. You are an example of how they will be in the future. Have a plan for how you want to raise them.

Emotional and Mental Health: Part of good health is your mental and emotional state of mind. I am not saying it is going to be a stress-free marriage. Every Marriage starts a little rocky. Those rocky obstacles are because you are still getting to know each other. You get to know each other while dating. However, now you are married. Most couples are always learning something new about their spouse after 30 years of Marriage.

Take the time to continue learning about your spouse. Use your partnership as a tool. Work together to manage the stress that comes your way. Explore healthy ways to work through conflicts before they become out of control. Always keep positive and look to the future together.

Sexual Intimacy and Affection: Enjoy each other's company. Find fun and creative ways to tell your spouse you love them. A simple kiss or a hug is a great way to show your affection. There are so many ways to show love to your spouse. A great idea is to hold hands. Try something bolder and more creative. Write them a love note. It sounds like something you would do while dating. However, it is still a fantastic way to show your love. Take it another step and hide it in the house where they can find it.

Most importantly, enjoy sexual intimacy. Making love brings meaning, pleasure, and satisfaction to your marriage. Enjoy being in each other's arms and find your favorite ways to say, *"I love you."*

I want you to stop reading this book. Take out a pen, get flowers, kiss your spouse, and do whatever you can think of to tell your spouse you love them. You should make them feel special. Surprise them and be creative. There is no limit to the number of times or ways you can show your love.

Take this time to see Appendix A: Marriage Assessment. This will be a great way to assess your Marriage. You can see the strengths and weaknesses of your Marriage. At the end of the assessment, you will decide on your Priority in each area I discussed in this chapter. It is essential to understand each other, what their priorities are, and not think about only yourself.

I encourage you to do this assessment every month for the first year. After that, continue to do it yearly to see how you are doing as a couple. Do not be afraid to do it more often. It is essential to know how you are doing and what you can do for your relationship to be more reliable.

Family Assessment

Your Marriage will have a substantial impact on your family. One day, you may have children. It does not matter if they are yours, adopted, or your spouses from a previous marriage. They are still your family. As you took the assessment for your Marriage, there was talk about children, and that is very important. Starting a family is a significant step in your lives.

Your children will have personalities from day one. Just like everything, they change. Those with a healthy marriage usually have a strong family. The trick is to have communication with your spouse and your children.

One thing I like to hear is when families have a weekly meeting. They call it a family meeting. Typically, it is at the beginning of the week. During this meeting, it gives the children a chance to have a voice. You get to know what they are doing during the week and can plan out your activities.

You show your spouse that you love them, you need to do the same for your children. It will help strengthen your family and your Marriage. Let your children see how strong you are as a couple. Work together to raise them. Most importantly, set the example they will follow as they get older and eventually get married themselves. Their future is in your hands and will be successful through your Marriage being successful.

Chapter 5: Communication

Communication is the key to any relationship. It is the main factor that holds a marriage together. Imagine going to the councilor, and the councilor did not pay attention to you; yet, you are there to communicate your problems. How effective would that be if you cannot talk about your issues? Communication is the key to working through marital issues. Do not assume your spouse can read your mind.

Your Spouse is Not a Mind Reader.

Learn to communicate regularly throughout your marriage. It is an essential part of the relationship. You are a team and should do everything as a team. In basketball, you work as a team and interact with the other members. It is the same with your team in marriage. How can we communicate in marriage?

Types of Communication for a Stronger Marriage

The four types of communication for strengthening your connection in marriage is defined as the act of transferring information from one place, person, or group to another. It is mainly composed of three factors; the sender, the message, and the receiver. One without the other two makes communication impossible. It is the process of sending verbal and non-verbal messages through your speech and body language, which includes the way you look, listen, move, and react to another person.

Communication gives meaning to your thoughts, goals, and appreciation for your spouse. It conveys your feelings, emotions, and dreams. This, by far, is the definition of communication that can be applied to every relationship.

Communication has always been a part of every related topic. After defining the term communication, you can tackle its role in a relationship and start exploring the different types that can strengthen your marriage or every relationship.

Most people agree that communication can make or break a relationship. Therefore, when spouses don't communicate effectively, they both experience frustration, anger, and resentment. On the other hand, couples who communicate well often experience less conflict, empathy, and real intimacy. Sometimes married couples expect their spouses to become mind readers, especially with women, to prove their true love and devotion. It is impossible and will lead to some significant problems. Through this, both partners expect themselves to fail and be disappointed. Therefore, effective communication is one of the critical aspects of marriage in which partners grow a more energetic and fruitful connection.

Partners who learn how to communicate effectively can make a beautiful union in marriage. It may not resolve all the marital problems each spouse has, but through proper communication, it will help steer some of them and keep them from becoming more significant issues. Some factors may or may not contribute to the aftereffects of communication in your marriage. Granted, they are based on the status of each relationship. Below are the types of communication that exist within different levels of married couples.

Newlyweds communicate differently from mature couples. Spouses during this stage have little arguments; yet, they talk about topics that do not require an exhausting emotional connection. They are still on the discovering stage showing their best behavior and self-control as often as they can. Newlyweds are always adapting to their situation as they were getting used to each other's routines, practices, traditions, and expectations.

The next level is the mature couples who communicate with each other freely and never hold out on things that bother them. They have gone through a lot of challenges. Once a problem arises, they already know what each other's perceptions are in these issues. They are on the same page and express this action frequently. They learn how to respect each other's boundaries, opinions, feelings, and characters after going through many hardships. They view their relationship as sacred and treat it with the utmost sensitivity since they have gone through a lot. They value their relationship more than anything else. Most of the time, couples in this stage communicate selflessly and make sure their partner is involved in most of their plans and future goals.

Effective communication is one key to a successful marriage, and it has become the expression of your feelings and emotions. Communicating with your partner is mandatory to keep a relationship more durable and make it last longer. Communication is a tool that holds a relationship together, and without it, a bond may crumble.

Your spouse wants to be recognized and appreciated. Simple gestures such as a thank you, note of appreciation, or any other way you can show them you are grateful for the things they do.

A good marriage seeks for an open exchange of emotions and goals in their relationship. Communication is one aspect of your relationship. Each of you should learn the skills of an effective communicator. Poor marriage communication changes the perspective of marriage. If spouses do not communicate effectively, the situation will display a different outcome. Conflict may occur, and negative emotions can intensify your problems. Poor communication could lead your marriage to a different level.

One scenario is when a husband is calling home to check up on his wife and would ask about plans for dinner. Their conversation did not take long, but this had been a part of his daily routine. These set-ups are informal, yet they contribute so much in making marriages work for years to come.

Joy has been married to a boy for almost 28 years. Through their years of marriage, they always woke up earlier than the kids as they consider this time of the day as their own. They like to talk about their plans for the day, matters about their daughters, what is for breakfast, work, and even politics. They talked about everything and exchange ideas throughout their conversations. Once the kids wake up, they go about their day as usual with limited communication left to brief and straightforward words. This routine lasted for only 30 minutes to 1 hour, which compares to the 24 hours of a day they have, but this does not mean they are infective communicators. During those moments, they share important things about their marriage and convey essential thoughts for a stronger relationship as they show the true essence of communication.

Couples who talk to each other depends on the length they have been together. There are formal, informal, or life-giving conversations. You will go about different kinds of communication that exist within a marriage and within a certain level. What are their contributions, how well do partners need to exercise them, and what are the effects on their spouses?

Informal Conversation: These conversations are part of your daily lives with your partner. They were composed mostly of random things and not important ones. These are conversations that happen every day and are the easiest to master. Couples started with these types of communication before they were married, the *"getting by knowing you"* talks where you talk about random things. They become part of your daily routine and were casual to each other. Informal communications are with your friends, peers, family, and coworkers. These conversations are free from rules, current organizational regulations, and other formalities. It only satisfies the social needs of people.

In a marriage, informal conversations are the most natural forms of communication. For example, we can say, *"How was your day?"* *"Fine. You?"* and *"Thanks! See you later."* It is passive, but not any close to be insulting. This may be small conversations or considered casual; however, these make up a part of communication every couple should practice. This may be only "small talk" for others but are essential to a marriage. They hold a relationship together by establishing a connection that does not require exhausting emotional strength just to pull through. They don't need a deep connection due to topics that were typically based on everyday scenarios.

Certain factors make up the reason for small talk in marriages. For example, couples who are busy doing something, perhaps work, chores, or looking after the kids might not find the time for a long conversation anymore, or they are exhausted after a long day at work. These conversations exist in every relationship, and it's normal.

Matters in this conversation can be discussed anytime and anywhere. They involve daily routines, present thoughts, and everyday scenarios. Perhaps, a wife is calling her husband to check on him as he mentioned earlier that he was about to go into an important meeting. This conversation is composed of favors, greetings, and discussions that don't need a follow-up. Another scenario is when a husband is checking on his wife after getting off work and would ask about dinner. Perhaps she is tired and wants him to get something on the way home or stop by the store because she needs something for dinner tonight. This may be a routine for some couples but nevertheless produces a vital factor in holding a marriage steady. This way, couples communicate through talking every day, even in simple words.

Administrative meetings: The word *"administrative"* is defined as people involved in carrying out duties, responsibilities, or required to complete a task. The organizational form of communication involves daily changes in the routine of each partner, their social obligations, decisions, and appointments. These are operational, which revolves around family matters and partner's day-to-day lives. Conversations like these are essential and discussed only once.

For example, a wife calls her husband to ask him to pick up the kids as she cannot do it. She is at the salon getting her hair done. She would not be able to make it on time by the time the kids get out of school. This is an excellent example of how plans can change.

Conversations like these are mainly composed of actions and favors. Administrative methods of communicating are purpose-driven, organized, and goal-oriented. To advertise in this manner requires a result in the end. The advantage of this medium is that your partner can process the daily lives of their family while making sure everything is in order. Especially with children, we can harness this skill and make them efficient and active parents.

Communicating in this manner is a sign of unhealthy relationships. For some couples, they only interact if they need something from each other, rather than interacting beyond this point, especially if it is something personal. Administrative settings are not driven by emotions; therefore, couples with an argument often talk this way.

Continuous communication in this manner can break a marriage apart as they no longer form a connection such romance. It slowly fades away, which leading to separation. These feel like an obligation rather than a free conversation with your partner.

This is the way divorced couples talk to each other. They only communicate for the benefit of their children and often share messages stating, *"we're done except if it concerns the children."* They conduct personal meetings only to discuss important matters and topics about their kid's school schedule and well-being. They do not talk about anything else except what is needed.

Challenges: Challenges can either make or break a relationship. All couples run into relationship problems, and how they deal with them says a lot about them. It is rare to see couples that do not have a few bumps in the road. Challenges are what makes a successful marriage. Challenges in married life can be a form of stress, financial problems, health issues, marital affairs, and children's well-being. It can be any sort of thing and can happen in every relationship. Thus, one way to strengthen a marriage is to talk about these problems. If you do not communicate, you will grow resent toward each other.

Healthy couples have learned how to manage these challenges and keep their love going. They communicate these challenges freely and establish points that could resolve their problems. They acknowledged the challenges are part of life, and accepting this will positively contribute to a healthy marriage. They see it as a growing experience individually and as a couple. Methods of communication involve sitting down with your partner and discussed the existing problem. You should share your opinions and come up with the best solution to the problem.

Involving your partner in every problematic situation they are facing is essential. Make sure you let your partner become aware of the decisions you make. You should also be honest, which is necessary and will contribute a lot. Fortunately, these marriage problems can be worked on. Aside from methods discussed here, there could be other ways to come out victorious in every challenging situation. It always depends on the couple's ability to overcome it.

Partners who face these challenges together will get a better chance to live a lifetime in marriage. They hang in there, tackle their problems, and learn how to work through the complexity of life. They become grateful and content with each other. They have become ready for whatever could go wrong, and they celebrate small victories. They mostly learn how to appreciate the diversity of life. Peace and happiness are usually the results of making it through successful challenges. After all, a couple gets married with their eyes open; therefore, there is no excuse to bring everything to the table when things get a little rocky.

Life-giving conversation: The other modes of communication are mostly reactive conversations that are motivated by some need or an event. This mode of contact should be dealt with proactively. Life-giving conversations have a proactive meaning. They are deep thoughts that are shared willingly by each couple. They involve intellectual beliefs and meaningful exchange. These are about getting to know your partner better and strengthening the bonds between you.

Curiosity often overrules by asking the spouse questions you've never asked before. You express gratitude by confiding in your spouse. Couples who practice this type of communication will express each other's fears, dreams, and past life. These topics are sensitive, and couples attempt to conceal them. However, the best way to turn past disappointments into future relationship success is through sharing these experiences with your new partner. All healthy and stable relationships begin with a heartbreak.

It is easy to see why meaningful conversations make a useful life. They show a commitment to understanding your partner's inner self. This will allow each partner to care more and to expand their understanding of their mate.

The Levels of Communication for a Stronger Marriage

Different factors can contribute to the effectiveness of communication within a marriage. These factors include the background of a husband, his childhood, or his environment, along with the wife's upbringing, beliefs, and experiences. A couple's unique style of communication develops over time. There are specific ways couples communicate with each other, and it depends on the length and in-depth of their relationship.

A couple who have been married for many years; may have gone through a lot of hardships stressing factors in their lives. It is like a fine wine; if tended to properly, it is getting better over time. They mature as a couple together and knows each other's personalities. They can communicate through mere look or hand signals, but the message comes across loud and clear. The level of communication depends on how deep a connection every couple has and how healthy their marriage is.

Let's look at different levels of communication that could strengthen a marriage. Take them to heart and apply each one to your relationship.

Necessary Information: This information is essential and a daily topic for couples. They are mostly related to facts and things needed for everyday lives. Expressions such as *"how are you doing honey, what do you plan to do today, or what is for dinner"* are mostly words that do not require explanation and follow up. These are questions and answers that are exchanged daily and are a normal part of the lives in a couple's relationship.

This information is being handled by couples every day and expresses indirectly. Necessary information does not require a more profound sense of emotions as they can only be express informally and openly. This may sound cliché for some but are the building blocks for a successful marriage.

Partnership: Partnership is central to a healthy marriage when an individual decides to share a particular goal in raising a family. As we go back to the definition of marriage, it is a union between two people who are bounded by love and affection. The alliance is composed of two people, the husband and the wife, who share one goal upon entering the relationship.

Shared communication is vital to couples, especially those with children. They must align their views, beliefs, and methods when it comes to raising and teaching kids. Communication is essential when kids are involved because this is the way kids will feel secure, knowing two parents are there for support and motivation. Aside from children's obligations, spouses share other responsibilities as well. Financial commitments, household chores, and decision making are some of the shared responsibilities. In a marriage, each person must think of others' interests and well-being. It is a partnership because it takes two people to make it work or destroy everything. Each partner does not own anything independently anymore. Anything that the other person owns can be the things that belong to the other spouse. After all, in most cases of the relationship, we can say two heads are better than one.

Conflict Resolution: Conflict resolution is a method or process that undertakes and facilitates the peaceful ending of conflict. The way married couples communicate to come up with a solution to a problem will determine the strength of their relationship.

Conflict in marriage is inevitable since we are all different individuals, and couples should face these conflicts with determination and teamwork. Marital conflicts are when something happens along the way that was not controlled and could harm the relationship. Partners should be able to work hand in hand to preserve their marriage in harmony. There are various strategies couples could focus on when solving a problem.

First, they should avoid or withdraw from conflict as much as possible. Take time to talk and find out what is wrong and what is the cause of the issue, whatever complications in the relationship can be resolved by talking, and having a deep understanding of the problems. Mix-up emotions happen to a couple who have a history of bad arguments over an issue that carries contrary after effects to their relationship. They must keep in mind not to pass by that road again.

Next, accommodate the best solution. You and your spouse should not compete but rather give way to somebody who can produce a better outcome. Both of you should take turns talking, and listening is a must. Collaborating is also useful in solving conflicts because each partner is assertive and cooperative. Each couple learns to allow each other to participate in decision making and co-create a possibility of sharing a solution you can agree upon.

Lastly, compromising on a solution will uplift ways to relate to your partner. Both of you need to say, *"let's call it a day and take part to engage in a favorable settlement."* Communication through this method is essential in every relationship. Couples who learn how to compromise will build trust, which is more durable than anything else. They trust each other to come up with a decision that can benefit both individuals.

The strength of a marriage is tested based on the couple's capability to solve and face the problem. The more hardships and stress they have undergone together, the stronger their relationship. There is a quote that I read somewhere, and it says, *"True to Life Love Story Does Not have Endings."*

Connection: We are all humans, and we are born to seek a relationship. Without regard to our spouse, we will result in as if something is lost and missing. Emotional connection is the bond that keeps people together. When you are emotionally connected, you build a relationship of strength, trust, and respect. You must be able to know your partner and put yourself in their situations. You will be able to tell that you are open with each other, and respecting each other's differences is a must.

Having an emotional connection to your partner means you can share anything with them to help you both grow. Context can also be in the form of physical connection through affection, eye contact, and body language. Some married couples do not realize this; unless they are not regularly connecting on an emotional level. Their marriage can turn sour.

There are some ways a couple can practice their emotional connection with each other. Try showing empathy, the ability to understand and share the feelings of the other. It is the capacity to understand or feel what the other person is feeling.

Next, caring for your spouse is a successful way of communication. This is the most powerful essence of communication; caring is equal to love. Before people engage in a relationship, they started caring first. Caring sets the tone on how couples communicate with each other. For example, if the wife does not care about her husband, she will not listen to any of the words he is saying. She will completely be eliminating the process of communication.

These various ways of showing a connection in a couple's life could determine the faith of a marriage. If couples practice emotionally connecting every day, it is like putting money into a savings account. They are investing in their relationship. The more they put in, the higher their love will grow.

Personal Revelation: This is a level of communication where couples share in the process of negative emotions, such as letting off steam of anger after a bad day at work or processing the violence related to the relationship. Anger should not be suppressed but instead discussed. You are also capable of violence, getting frustrated at some point, and a link is not only about romance and positive affection. It is also about going through problems together.

Communicating your negative emotions to your partner does not indicate you are weak but rather strong enough to let others witness your fragility. By exercising this, married couples approach a deeper level of communication by showing vulnerability. This is showing your inner self to your partner without taking much prejudice and judgments from him or her.

This type of communication is about letting your spouse into your world. Managing negative emotions tells more about a person. Couples who go through this together put their relationship on a different plain or into a different level.

Intimate Communication: These are deep affection, expressions of love, and whispers of *"I love you."* These are the ways of intimacy that only couples exercise. These words and actions build closeness that binds a healthy marriage.

Privacy is being comfortable with your partner and showing them your inner self, your fears, more profound thoughts, and deepest desires. Intimacy is bringing your marriage to the level of a true partnership.

Some couples find it hard to communicate intimately for various reasons. For instance, the wife comes from a conservative family. She learned that discussing topics such as "sex" is not an open topic, so when she enters a marriage, she finds it difficult to discuss this topic. In this scenario, if the husband is not aware of his wife's upbringing, then the matter will likely lead to a misunderstanding. Another example is when people with anxiety problems and body image issues will sometimes have difficulty being comfortable with their spouses.

A spouse can help their partner by being encouraging and expressing their love clearly. A professional can also promote this partner to learn to feel more comfortable about themselves.

Intimate conversations are a part of marriage and are essential in keeping a marriage alive. Also, having intimate conversations imply that the person is special, and you appreciate their company. The private discussion of a couple brings their relationship to a deeper connection. When partners have a healthy level of intimacy, they will find it easy to talk about these sensitive subjects.

Understanding these types of communication is essential in a healthy marriage. Knowing when to implement these different types of communication in a marriage can go a long way in strengthening the bonds between husband and wife and enhances personal satisfaction.

This is only a guide for couples who had gone through a lot already. This does not guarantee effective results in terms of solving a conflict or perhaps makes a marriage last longer. Keep in mind, every wedding is different, and every couple is unique.

The strength and the length of a relationship will depend on the ability of the couple to fix any problem. Turn a disagreement around, and gain enough patience to continue. This guide will only work if you put your mind to it and do your part. It is in your hands to make it work and strengthen your marriage.

Chapter 6: Building Blocks of Trust

Everyone has a goal of a successful marriage with the hope for a better future. Part of that marriage requires trust. It is hard to make it through marriage without faith. You must trust in your partner. They are the ones by your side.

Trust does not also come easy. It takes work. Many people do not give it away like candy. It is not free to consider if it is not given to you first. Once your partner confides in you with complete trust, and you break that trust, it is tough to get back. However, it is not impossible. It takes work. In the end, your hard work will pay off as they trust you again.

Most of us do not have the tools to build a house. However, everyone has the tools for building trust in your marriage. You just may not realize it.

The Building Blocks to A Successful Marriage

Marriage is a process in which two people are love. They trust each other, are honesty, and all workings of what it takes to make a relationship last. For the most part, marriage is what binds two people who are in love and wants to build a future together.

Marriage carries all the sacrifices a relationship should have; to include but not limited to, forgiveness, strength, and love. For a successful marriage, it is more than romance. It takes a lot of work to communicate without undergoing conflict, problems, and temptation.

To keep up with the needs of a marriage is also hard work, compromises, and to learn to respect your partner's needs. This can be difficult, especially at the beginning of the relationship. Therefore, the levels of marriage exist.

Over time, a marriage develops and grows, which every relationship stays on a different level depending on the learnings they achieve. The longer the marriage lasts, the more mature the couples are. They endure many hardships as they are healthier for them. They will grow not only as a couple but also as an individual.

There is no perfect recipe for marriage nor an ideal person to do the job. Every marriage has its own pace, strength, and depends on perseverance to make a marriage work. This will define their marriage. Surely, love is yet one of the first ingredients to a healthier marriage. As mentioned earlier, a marriage is made up of everything that makes a relationship last. Marriage is only one aspect of a successful relationship.

Love is the key to opening the door of every relationship, upon entering it, you will likely meet the other factors that a relationship needs to be tackled to build a stable house of marriage. Therefore, I want to introduce the building blocks for marriage to become successful. Learning them might help a couple who struggles to stabilize their marriage.

You will embark on a journey of learning the building blocks that could create a way to a healthy marriage, maintaining it, strengthen it, and even make it last a lifetime. These building blocks are the foundations of the union that takes away those negative factors, such as irritants, missteps, and quarrels. These essential blocks of a successful marriage or relationship are Open Dialogue, Trust, and Vulnerability. Let us take the step of getting to know each one of them. They are the reasons why trust exists in a relationship and how to allow for it to continue to exist.

Open Dialogue: The first of the three building blocks of a successful marriage is Open Dialogue. The word *"dialogue"* means to take part in a conversation or discussion to resolve a problem. This makes open communication between couples possible.

Communication between spouses should not only be limited to asking how each other's day went or what is for dinner. It is more than just talking. It should not be limited to discussing only topics such as children, the household, activities, vacations, extended families, and the weather. When it comes to open dialogue, couples should also talk about the current status of their relationship, about romance, ways to rekindle their relationship, and intimacy.

Most couples are often fearful that their partner will reject or abandon them every time they will share their true feelings of what they need. They feel by sharing their opinions, and it can create disagreements, conflict, and even establishing high expectations for their partner. This strategy often causes internal conflict or create resentments that often leads to marital problems.

The strategy of open dialogue is about making a meaningful and heartfelt connection with your partner. Telling them what you feel is what starts a relationship in the first place. The words *"I love you"* start because of a conversation that is deeper than any communication. Hence, a good marriage lies in how couples communicate with each other. Openness is about sharing your deeper self to your partner, which translates your words to how you feel with another person. Thus, creating an emotional bond that increases desirable affection and intimacy.

Deep conversation is what differentiates a marriage or a causal relationship. There are certain things that only a married couple could understand; meaning, you are likely to be married if you have more of a deeper connection to your spouse than anybody else.

Open dialogue has four patterns: first is a connection through a more in-depth level; second is venting about somebody or something; third is solving a problem together, and last is considering the person you are communicating with to fix the problem for you. However, it is not only about adjusting your questions for someone or having somebody rant your feelings out, but rather, it is about sharing strength with your partner, which is the best in any relationship. It is discussing the problems, so both the met and unmet needs and issues are solving together. It is about talking about the future, dreams, and needs. Open dialogue is essential in marriage because through this, you'll grow as a person who cares and is cared about.

Trust: Trust is more than just being emotionally and physically faithful. Trust is more than a factor that keeps a marriage healthy. It can make or break a relationship. For others, the word trust can be connected to fidelity. Fidelity is showing continuous support, loyalty, and faithfulness to someone. Unfailingly commitment to your partner makes your relationship grow even more reliable.

There are a lot of ways how each partner can show their trust for each other. For instance, trusting your partner means you give them freedom, but with limitations, you believe them to follow these certain boundaries. This could prevent you from having disagreements. It is about trusting your partner that they will respect and honor these boundaries you set in your relationship. Also, by giving your partner the benefit of the doubt means trusting them that even after a mistake, they will still make it up to you by fixing what they did.

Trust is forgiveness. Trust is understanding your partner after they sinned against you. Trusting your partner means they can become your confidante, someone who listens with no judgment yet will face criticism. You are trusting your spouse to support you and empathetically listen to you when they need your attention. Supporting your partner means trusting them. You believe in your partner to reach their goals and aspirations.

Building trust is hard, yet can easily be broken. The best way to build trust is by honoring your words in small and more significant things. For example, if you tell your partner, you'll be home at a specific time, you need to be at home exactly when you said. Sometimes some circumstances prevent you from honoring your words. If this happens, you need to be honest with your partner and make them aware of your situation; if your partner trusted you, they would understand. Being honest is showing integrity and respect towards yourself and your partner.

These building blocks come in many forms. Trust may be general in terms of meaning, but in marriage, it only means one thing. It can be something that could make or break your relationship.

Vulnerability: Vulnerability is frequently mistaken for weakness. For it means showing your fears, what causes you pain, and makes you sensitive. This can be difficult, especially for those who have had past relationships, abusive origin, or a challenging childhood. All these could lead the person to show toughness as a front. It is only shared by a person through their strength and independence after going through something. It is hard for them to show vulnerability and share their weakness to others. It is hard enough to share sensitive matters with your partner only to have those feelings be taken for granted; therefore, the aspect of being healthy is personal. By putting faith into someone as your partner, you trust them to see when you are the most vulnerable. A healthy marriage yields stronger emotions.

A meaningful connection can only keep on working if both partners are willing to express these tough, sensitive, anxiety-inducing emotions, and trust that your partner will accept them with love. You need to give more time and a lot of patience to break the hard shell of sensitivity. A person with a difficult childhood or an abusive past does not let people in so quickly. It will take hard work and perseverance to understand what your partner went through.

Among the three building blocks of marriage, this is the hardest one to master. It encompasses open dialogue and trust. To be vulnerable, you need to trust your partner will respect your weaknesses and have an open conversation to talk about things that are sensitive to you. The essence of being a human is to connect with others. Therefore, marriage was created.

People are meant to be with others. You are expected to connect with someone. The vulnerability exists to serve as a driving force of connection between the two of you.

Relationship Help: Building Blocks of Trust and Intimacy

The stereotype of the word *"intimacy"* often leads people to think it means a sexual relationship with your partner. Yet intimacy is not all about sexual purposes. In a relationship, intimacy involves feelings of emotional connections to your partner by accepting their attitudes, ability to love, more profound thoughts, and emotional baggage. Often, intimacy with couples involves taking psychological risks wherein they share their details and stories. Privacy and trust go together hand in hand. A couple can only become intimate if they trust each other.

Commitment: The nature of your obligations can be seen in every person's life. Commitment will come in different forms, such as your career, your family's well-being, or your daily plans and goals. It has the determination and patience by doing a series of actions to achieve a positive outcome. Commitment is goal-oriented, which depends on the person's value of goals and commitment.

In love and dating, with the presence of media and technology, relationship labels come and go like season changes. Confirming a relationship status seems to be difficult these days for this generation. They enjoy being involved in an open relationship instead of committing to one that is more serious. These open relationships make it more comfortable, and no deeper connection is needed. This generation is impulsive, and so are their decisions when it comes to a relationship. They prefer not connecting further to the person they are seeing; thus, when things go wrong, they will be out in the woods in no time. There will not be any regrets because a connection is not formed in the first place. Therefore, the importance of commitment is gradually slowing. However, for others, being in a relationship is a sign of maturity, especially if it is through committing to the one they love. Some view commitment as a value of trust.

A sign of close relationships and couples who are committed to each other often grows positively within you. The main goal of commitment is to have a clear sense of security from your partner. They trust each other and will not take part in any affairs or situations that can harm or destroy their relationship. They believe in their partner to share sensitive matters that give meaning to their marriage.

Commitment overrules love when it comes to maintaining a healthy connection and will keep a relationship going strong. It is why couples decide to stay even after a significant disagreement, and it is through sacrifices by you and your spouse to provide for their needs. It is what drives us to keep pushing on and help each other even after a severe meltdown.

Commitment stabilizes a relationship. Every couple decides to pursue a relationship, work to make it happen, struggles through the hard times, and strives to keep it healthy. Responsibility is one of the significant aspects that makes up a healthy relationship with love and trust. Without these three, a serious relationship may crumble. Commitment is the will to stay together and be strong for each other.

Once a couple decides to commit to each other, it is where the trust builds. The individual will trust their partner enough to share a part themselves. They believe in them enough to invest their time and affection for you. They are inspired and set routines. You will find looking at the bigger picture is helpful and keeps you on track with your goals. Planning the future together is a key to seeing yourself together for many years to come.

Part of being committed to each other is transparency. Transparency shows your partner that you trust them and will strengthen your commitment to one another. One way of explaining this is through exchanging usernames and passwords to all your accounts, as this is considered the ultimate form of trust.

My wife and I practice transparency throughout our years of marriage. We each have different computers. However, the same accounts are on each computer with the passwords saved. Therefore, it does not matter what equipment we are on, we both have access to all the accounts. These accounts include E-mail, Social Media, and messengers. Even our phones are accessible to each other. There are no passwords to get into them, and they are always visible to the other person. These are small and simple ways to show commitment through transparency.

Reliability: People or things that are reliable can be trusted to work well or behave in the way you want them to be. Relationships are built on trust; without it, they will not last long or stay healthy. Being reliable to your partner is trusting them enough to keep their word and being by each other's sides when things go wrongs. They can be counted on when the activity becomes difficult.

In a relationship, being reliable means maintaining the same momentum each partner has on the first day they met until the next level of their relationship. It forges deeper relationships and supports the level of trust they have, creating a security control for both partners. However, unreliability can take a variety of forms. Perhaps, it can be in the way of being late for every meeting, or it is taking longer for you to reply to an urgent text message. It may be little things but certainly can break off a relationship.

This form of unreliability can have severe and adverse effects on a person's sense of security and self-esteem. If left untreated, this lack of reliability can be damaging to the relationship because it is making it more challenging to trust someone. These small details of unpredictable actions can accumulate into a severe significant problem. Together, these instances can add up to become our perception of how trustworthy a person is, how you can rely on them, and feel secure around them.

Trust is about believing in your partner when they make decisions that impact your relationship. It is trusting them that they will do and choose the right thing in every hard situation they were facing. It is a general feeling of putting your belief in them: an assurance that your relationship will endure and become stronger.

Dealing with an unreliable partner takes hard work and patience. Every partner should have an open conversation and be honest with each other. If the actions of your partner are affecting the relationship, then it is time to address the situation and let your partner be aware of it rather than put it under the bed. Communicate to your partner what is upsetting you, treat them in a manner that they would understand, and keep an open mind for criticism. Always be free to hear your partner's frustrations, and never let them feel you are not listening. After all, being reliable is still being there.

Consistency: During courtship, often, the man, when pursuing a girl, does every desirable thing he can think of from giving flowers, sending love notes on every special occasion, calling her every day, or making excuses to see her daily. He makes every note in the book when pursuing a girl. However, after years of being in a relationship, these gestures are slowly fading away. Those love notes fade, the special occasions had been forgotten, and those actions of pursuit had been lost along the way. What causes them is most couples become comfortable with each other that they do not feel the need to connect anymore. There might be factors affecting consistency during the span of marriage.

For some, having children right after a marriage reduces the time for date nights and celebrating special occasions. After getting married, couples face responsibility such as financial obligations of a family, decision-maker, and breadwinner, which, most of the time, take the word romance and consistency out of the picture. Others are viewing marriage as an endpoint of courtship and pursuing.

Consistency often gets left behind in a relationship, love, and other things that get overruled. However, the importance of unity does not get overruled. In marriage, without a sense of connection, it will likely fall apart. Connecting every day as husband and wife is essential for a wedding to be healthy. One example of this is a husband still takes his wife on a date for their anniversary. Also, a man sends flowers and letters to his wife even after five kids and without occasions. These are only small gestures, but if done consistently, it will make a relationship even more reliable.

Being consistent means something that stays the same, is done the same way, or looks the same. Consistency in marriage is critical, and it means checking on one another regularly. It means being there when you are needed. Upon entering a relationship, you start building a lifetime together; you start creating good memories and pulling strings together to keep a marriage from falling apart; thus, without consistency, you will lose the progress and find yourselves starting over again.

Acceptance: Entering a relationship is accepting everything it has to offer. Full recognition of your partner means welcoming all the different parts of who they are, even the traits that seem to be challenging. The importance of receipt in a relationship is embracing everything about your partner, even the ones that carry the most burdensome baggage. Perhaps, your partner had been in an abusive relationship before, or they experience a specific trauma caused by a tragedy.

These negative experiences can impact a person's life and the way they live. Some of them adapt the change after a tragedy happened. For example, when your partner does not sleep with lights off anymore. When you accept your partner, you acquire their fears, bad past relationships, and tragic events that happened to your loved one.

You need to realize and understand that not all people's experience is the same. Therefore, entering this kind of relationship takes an amount of affirmation and patience. Providing them the feeling of security and comfort that shows that you can accept the way they are. It takes a certain amount of acceptance towards your partner when there are things you cannot change. You cannot expect a relationship without a certain higher-level degree of recognition.

It also takes acceptance to comprehend the changes that surround your relationship. Often with the different perceptions and personalities of every person involved in a relationship, challenges are likely to occur. Each needs to be selfless at times and accept the things that cannot be changed. They need to grasp that some things will not go the way they wanted, and a healthy relationship understands the nature of these challenges and chose to fight over it.

A relationship becomes more reliable and happier once every couple started to accept these challenges rather than ignoring them. This is recognizing the person for who they are and being attentive to every disagreement in your relationship.

How Do We Build Trust in a Relationship?

Trust is relying on a person's words, ideas, and support without any biased and unsolicited thoughts. It is the feeling of being secure, and it mirrors the whole character of a person. It creates a wholesome connection between people and, most notably, between relationship partners. Trust is a foundation that builds honesty, integrity, and a healthy relationship.

It is integral to practice trusting your partner in every situation. Trust is giving your partner the liberty to do what they want only with limitations you both agree upon. Trusting your partner means expecting them to abide by those rules. It is the faith you have with someone that they will always remain loyal to you and love you. It is through trusting that each partner overcomes difficult situations together. Trust is key to a long-lasting relationship.

Be true to your word and follow through with your actions: Say what you mean and mean what you say as trust is earned. The point of building trust is for others to believe what you say by displaying integrity, honesty, and giving reassurance to people. You must be taken by people as a person who always keeps his word not only in more significant gestures but also in small ways.

For instance, you were applying for a job and was prompted by the company to have your interview at a specific time, you then reassure them you will comply; which, you somewhat did the moment the meeting came. This is an essential value for a person to absorb, helps a person to grow, and mature as an individual. You also contribute to the well-being of others.

Being true to your words make people rely on you for support and personal favors. They will trust you enough to share their affairs and be part of their support system. They will come running into you when things get complicated because they know you can be count on. It is essential to practice integrity and honesty towards other people.

This can also be applied to a relationship. In marriage, you need to trust your partner that they will only do actions that will benefit your companionship and not the other way around. You need to give them the benefit of the doubt that even without your presence, they will only do things that are not beyond the boundaries you set. You need to do everything you can to treat the trust as fragile as possible. Trust is the main foundation of a relationship that connects both of your inner selves.

Once trust is gone, partners can no longer continue a relationship. For it is integral to a happy and fulfilling love story. Building trust is not only about making the promises you are unable to keep but also to the ones you did not hold. Once the trust is broken, it will be hard to build it back; especially, with people who pick up grudges after a misunderstanding. It will take time to earn that trust again.

Learn how to communicate effectively: Communication is the process of transmitting a message from a receiver to a sender, which is a process that is crucial to the well-being of a relationship. Poor communication can turn a connection into a misfit, and it can create disagreements and conflicts; which, ultimately leads to separation.

Communication is not just about talking; it's about creating a connection to your partner about your inner-self, thoughts, plans, and aspirations. Excellent communication includes giving a clear message to your partner about your commitment to them, your affection, and your future projects together.

Communicating correctly in a relationship is also building trust; it allows you and your partner to take risks together and eliminate any doubts of negative things that could happen. If you have no problem expressing yourself, you'll find working out your disagreements to be secure and with no hassle.

Certain things can help you become an effective communicator to your partner. First, you need to be a listener, and it's not just about talking but also learning how to listen well. Next, paying attention to the body language of your partner. If a person is upset, they usually skip the talking and start showing it through body language. Find common ground when you find yourself in a conflict with your partner, considering this could help both of you to come up with solutions that benefit everybody. These are only some of the many factors that can help you become an effective communicator to your partner and others.

Remind yourself that It takes time to build and earn trust: In building trust, it takes a lot of patience and commitment to make a person trust you. It is a daily work of progress, especially for someone who has a hard time believing people. Sometimes for other people, trust is not as common as other things; hence the famous saying *"trust is earned."*

Do not make the mistakes of expecting too soon because earning trust is daily work. Take things one step at a time, do not rush the process but rather enjoy the journey of earning the trust of the person you care so deeply about. In a relationship, nothing can come off so quickly, not even the love you have for each other. It will always go through a process until achieving a positive result. You just must be patient with yourself and with your partner.

Take time to make decisions and think before acting too quickly: This strategy teaches you how to say *"No"* on things that do not favor you. Always remember to think before you act, especially with the decisions concerning your relationship. Never haste making a promise when you can't keep it anyway. Never put a person in a difficult situation because you promise them something that you cannot comply with. It will not only ruin your reputation but also decreases your chances of earning people that you can trust.

Always take time to decide and think before acting. It is still essential to have a clear mind before making an important decision. This way, you can explore your options and weigh them by first taking time off before choosing what to decide. Although small choices can be made quickly, important decisions must be made carefully.

Be vulnerable — gradually: For a healthy balanced relationship, an open, honest, and authentic communication must exist within partners. Being vulnerable is being transparent to your partner through thoughts and emotions. It is letting your partner see you not only physically but also knowing you emotionally. Both partners should develop a bond with each other that is much tighter than decades of small talk, and it is because they must be vulnerable with each other.

Building trust takes confidence in opening yourself to your partner, talking about your fears, embarrassing past, hurtful incidents, and showing parts of yourself that are not pretty and makes you feel weak. However, vulnerability is not just about you feeling vulnerable or being too ugly on the inner side of yourself, and vulnerability is accepting these limitations and turning them into your strength. Therefore, in a relationship, seeing these weaknesses of your partner means they are trusting you by letting you in. Every partner must be understanding in handling this hurtful past or scary fears. Trust your partner to undergo the process with you, gradually and safely.

Remember the role of respect: In a healthy relationship, partners are equal, which means that neither partner has authority over the other; thus, respecting each other is essential. It balances everything in a relationship that coincides between partners; for example, their differences in personalities.

Having respect exist in a relationship, both partners accept each other for who they are even beyond their differences and opposite personalities. Conflict may be settled quickly and preventing it from turning disagreement into the worst fight if respect rules within. For instance, a husband will never become abusive towards his partner if he respects her. Respecting your partner means setting limitations and abiding them to prevent yourself from hurting them.

Respect builds trust, honesty, and integrity in a relationship. It sees through the good and learns to accept the bad. It is necessary for a healthy relationship, for it means you recognize your partner as a whole person.

Chapter 7: Tools for a Solid Intimate Relationship

Every situation we face in a relationship calls for a different approach. Yet, in my years of Marriage, I found that there is no permanent solution or magic spell in the relationship. You must learn to choose the things that will benefit both of you to fully share your minds, hearts, bodies, and souls. We are each individual, so the level of your intimacy is different from other people. However, these are my top-secret tools. They will add spice and excitement to your lifelong dedication.

Be Positive

Always be positive as they say; there is still sunshine behind every dark cloud. Difficult situations always happen. Have a positive outlook on these situations will help you get through them. They will not last forever, and they will soon pass. Think of it as a test of your endurance through marriage. You can always find good results in every bad situation and consider them as blessings to help strengthen your marriage. You will see more of a precise picture of your partner in stressful situations; thus, you can still learn. When under pressure, you will begin to see the real person you married.

By learning to accept your partner in life, you will find out more about the person you are married too. Your partner will surely be amazed on how you have climbed the mountains together without the hype of fighting. Isn't that thrilling?

Appreciating Each Other

Learn to compliment and build up each other. I do not agree that romance and all its strategies end while in a relationship. The longer couples live together, the thrill and excitement will continue. The secret is always complimentary. Meaning, be honest about what you like with your partner and be gentle on what you do not like.

Your partner will feel loved and satisfied when you are grateful for their positives and soft on the negatives and accepting their flaws. Being gentle in words when correcting does not involve any special skills. Soft words can do magic and turn away wrath. The bottom line is the tone of your voice and being honest with your words and actions. Make both compliments and corrections from the heart. You will grow together in love and strengthen your relationship.

Soft Words Can Do Magic and Turns Away Wrath.

Share and make memories, hobbies, interests, and explore life to the fullest. Time spent with your spouse creates a moment to have a deeper connection. These memories will last a lifetime.

Appreciating your spouse is like enjoying your favorite lemonade. For example, I work at home, and most of the time, I am in front of the computer. My wife will cook my favorite meal and bring it to me. This simple gesture makes me appreciate her more.

It does not matter how big or small the act is. Instead, it is about the way it is done. Life, after all, is full of beautiful things to appreciate.

Submission

Being submissive may sound so dogmatic, yet it involves denying one self-principles and attitudes toward a healthier relationship. As long it does not violate any laws and philosophies in life, we also define submission as being a helper, supporter, and lover to your partner. It will streamline the boundaries as time goes by and leads to a relaxing, harmonious, and content life together.

There are no perfect relationships, but to an imperfect couple trying to submit to one another is an ideal picture of a lasting union. When you submit to your partner in a good way is healthy and creates a beautiful thing in your relationship. When you are married, you have already submitted it to your partner and do not stop there. Marriage is a learning process. You must learn everything there is about your spouse. You must give everything you have to your relationship.

Forgive Yourself Before You Can Forgive Others

Before you can forgive others, you must forgive yourself. I call this, *"Forgive to Forgive."* We came from different family cultures. There will be times where we have caused hurt and awkward moments that made us bitter. Then it's time to let go by forgiving yourself. Through forgiveness, you will experience inner peace, so apply forgiveness and let go of the things which cause you pain. Focus on the now and realize the choices you have.

Positively, these molded you in such a way to become healthier and adaptive in the same situation. Forgiving yourself will give you the capability to move on from the hurt in your past. Use your mistakes as an inspiration to learn and grow better, then replace them with positive thoughts. You will also learn to forgive your partner, and you will understand how to be better involved in the current situation. Nobody's perfect. In some way or another, we fail, yet by forgiving and learning through them, we become better and not bitter.

Be Unpredictable

The magic stays the same when ordinary things become extraordinary. Do things randomly and unplanned. Be resourceful and innovative to add spice along the way. Jogging or walking together with your partner becomes memorable when a rose or flowers await at the end of your journey of the day.

A romantic dinner at home can be made as a surprise when you make it a special occasion. Anything under the sun can be turned into a situation with a different outcome can be thrilling to your partner. Anyways, life is full of surprises, and why not always be magical!

When we were dating, I would take a trip to see my wife. I would surprise her with flowers and her favorite chicken dinner. Knowing I was still working, I would take the time during my break just to see her and spend time together. Being unpredictable is one way to bring romance and excitement into the relationship.

Outside of the Bedroom is the Start of Foreplay

Most people think that foreplay needs to be in the privacy of your own home. You need to understand the expectations of your partner. Men and women spell intimacy in different ways. A simple hug or gentle kiss can create intimacy, allowing them to feel safe and share their emotions with each other. Through the power of an intimate relationship, you will feel more love towards your partner and less being alone.

For men, it is straight forward that intimacy is spelled, S. E. X. They think that familiarity with their partner is sex and nothing else. They do not see it as anything else. Men are more about the physical aspect, such as touch, feeling, kissing, and hugs. For example, I feel closer to my wife through a simple touch, kiss, or hug to tell me she is thinking about me.

Women view intimacy differently. To a woman, intimacy is spelled as T.A.L.K. For example, my wife enjoys the time we spend drinking tea and talking about anything under the sun. Women feel that it is more intimate to talk and figure things out. They value communication more about privacy. They value open communication.

In some situations, the roles are reversed. Sex for men is as essential as talking for women. They feel loved and cared about in the relationship. However, It works both ways. You need to understand the other person. For you to increase intimacy in your relationship, you must understand their needs.

A woman wants to be swept off their feet through romance. They want a lover who understands them and makes them the priority. At the same time, men want a woman who is willing to be there for them. Each partner wants the same thing. They want a lover who understands them and supplies their needs.

We cannot fix all our problems through sex. Sex alone will not create intimacy. The same goes for only talking. Talking will not create an intimate relationship. Instead, combine them through foreplay and show your passion towards each other.

Welcome Expectations that Are Realistic

Have realistic expectations and welcome them with an open mind. It takes time for a woman to be emotionally ready to take things to the bedroom. Unlike men, they can go to the bedroom and immediately be prepared for some fun.

It is essential to understand each other. Men need to be patient; women need to be ready. Good things come to those who wait. Accepting those differences are the reasons why you are together in the first place. Enjoy and cherish them.

As you go throughout the day, you can leave short love notes of appreciation for each other. There are tricks to bringing in the intimacy you desire. Men should take advantage of the waiting and create the entire day full of romance. Better yet, do it every day. Make it a routine and enjoy the journey of intimacy.

Men should be passionate about love and care for their wives. As women start to feel love and security from their spouses, they are driven to sexual arousal. They feel the need to be with you and have a desire for sexual intimacy.

There will be times when sexual intimacy will not meet your expectations. That is the time to talk. Find out what your partner needs. Ask questions and find what is missing. You need to fulfill the needs of your partner to have the desired expectations.

Think of it like a math problem that needs to be solved daily, where you are trying to get both sides of the equation to be equal. When you have a secure emotional connection, you will have a good sexual relationship and a strong foundation.

Ladies – Your Man is Important

You should always respect your man giving him time and thinking about his wants and needs. They need to feel needed by their wives, who think they are superheroes. Men need their wives to always stand by them in everything they

do, which includes their need for sexual desires. This is part of who they are.
When you are married, you make a commitment to stand by their side. When
this need is not met, they will start to feel they are not needed or wanted in the
relationship. In some cases, men seek for that attraction and focus to other vices
to the point of venturing outside the marriage commitment. You want to stop that
from happening.

Do you find yourself putting your husband down? Do you call him every name in
the book and tear him down? Do you misspend your savings? Do you set aside
his ideas and opinions instead of listening to him? If your answer is yes to any of
these questions, why do you expect him to be tender and consider you?

If you want to see your expectations of being treated right by his tenderness, you
must give him the respect he desires. You must honor him. You made a
commitment to each other in marriage. Give him the respect he deserves, and
he will fulfill everything you want. It is about giving and taking. You give what he
desires, and he will give it back to you. You are a team. Work together as a
team to fulfill your desires and strengthen your marriage as one.

Men – Your bride is Everything

There is a big problem with many relationships. We just talked about the women
and what they need to do. However, I have seen relationships where the men
treat their bride as an object that will perform when they want her too. Your wife
is not a machine with an on and off button to fulfill your primary wants and needs.
She is not an object or a piece of meat. The way you treat each other is a two-
way street. You reap what you sow. Like in love, how you treat your wife will
bring forth blessings or consequences.

Men must start to understand their wives. You should cherish her and treat her
with respect. She is everything to you and serves your undivided affection.
Instead of taking her directly to the bedroom, you should try talking to her
instead. Ask her about what she did for her day. Get to know her likes and
dislikes. You will learn something new about each other every day you are
married through communication you bring into the relationship. Share with her
your dreams and listen to her as she does the same. Pour out your heart. This
is the way to get closer to her.

If you want to take it to the bedroom, start outside of the bedroom with her heart.
You do not want to go straight to it. The desire will not be in it. You must work
towards it through communication outside of the bedroom. Show her how much
you care about her feeling and her heart.

Your wife does a lot at home. In my family, I work while she stays home and
takes care of the chores, washes the dishes, cooks for the family, arranges the
furniture, keeps the house clean, takes care of the children, etc. Face it, you go

to work so you can provide a stable home for your family. Show her how much you appreciate her by helping when you can. I tell my wife how much she means to me and thank her every day. She does so much to make it easier for me to do my job. That is why, when she needs help with something, I do it without questions.

I want you to go to chapter 8. Look under the heading for the *"Appreciation List"* and start making a list of all the things you appreciate about your wife. It is never too late to show your appreciation for her. The only wrong choice you could make is to never do it.

Find Your Sexy

You should make intimacy a priority in your relationship. Do not just say, *"we will make love tonight."* However, you may need to schedule it on your calendar. The point, it should have a high priority. Making love is essential in every marriage.   Life gets busy. It can be hard to schedule it into your busy lives once you start having a family. Yet, it is still vital. Do it regularly.

Remember, a physical aspect is how you bond with your husband. Men do not forget; it is not all about you. Listen to your wives and let them direct you during sexual intimacy. Learn from them as they will learn from you. This is a time for exploration of each other's bodies.

Sexual intimacy should be enjoyed by you both. There may be times when you are not in the mood. Maybe you are only having sex to please your partner. If this is the case, it is better to sit down and talk. You cannot gain the desire for intimacy in the relationship. However, you do need to make it a part of your regular lives.

You need to invest in each other and their needs. Never hold grudges. Always open that line of communication. Men, if your wife does not want sexual intimacy, do not withdraw. Women, if your husband wants sexual intimacy and you are not in the mood, communicate with him and let him know what is on your mind. You should never distance yourself from each other.

What is Your Language of Love?

Each person has a different language of love. It is like going to China and trying to speak English. You cannot understand each other unless they speak English, or you talk in Chinese.

Love has its own language. Dr. Gary Chapman has done a lot of research on the subject and has determined that the expression of love can be divided into five different areas. Each of these areas is defined; however, the imagination is the limit. That means, regardless of the language your spouse speaks, the only limitation to showing your love in that language is your imagination. This can be the key to your marriage lasting for a lifetime and creating that unbreakable bond.

Words of Affirmation: Do not assume your spouse knows how you feel. If their love language is Word of Affirmation, they probably do not know. You should tell them. They need to hear it. Do not stop telling them. In fact, make it a goal to let them every day.

The language of Word of Affirmation needs encouragement. They need to hear they did a good job. When there is a lack of motivation, it will stop them from achieving all the positive things they can do. You will find the words of encouragement will bring out the best in your spouse.

If your spouse's language of love is *"Words of Affirmation,"* encourage them and tell them how much they mean to you and your family. They need to hear it.

Physical Touch: There is no secret or magic behind the physical touch. It has shown love and affection from the beginning. However, to your spouse, whose love language is through physical contact, it means so much more. Through simple things like a kiss, a hug, warm embraces, holding hands, and intercourse will tell your partner you love them.

One thing to remember, not all touches have the same meaning. Some contacts may give more pleasure to your spouse than others. The best coach is your spouse. Listen to them, and they will guide you in the way physical touch will show your love and care about them.

Be careful with the way you touch your partner. There may be touches that irritate them. This will give the opposite effect and will show them you do not care about their feels or needs. Do not think your spouse will enjoy the same touches you enjoy. Communication is everything. You are the guide for your partner while they are the guide for you. Listen to each other, both verbally and nonverbally.

Quality Time: When your love language is *"Quality Time,"* you need to focus on your spouse. This does not mean watching television together. A movie occasionally would be ok. However, you should turn off the tv and talk with each other. Try having a date night or taking a walk. Spend time together.

Through quality time, you will share your thoughts, desires, feelings, and experiences. My wife and I enjoy looking at old pictures and videos together. They bring back fond memories. We laugh, joke, and relive those experiences repeatedly.

Acts of Service: Through marriage, you learn to work as a team. Your spouse may take care of the house, children, and cooking. This does not mean you should not help. Simple acts of service to your spouse will show them you care about their needs.

Acts of Service will need thoughtful planning, your time, energy, and effort. When done with a positive heart, it will show them how much you care and love them. Do not do it because they ask you for help. Do it, because you see it needs to be done and you would like to help. A great idea is to do the tasks without being asked and surprise them.

Gifts: We give gifts for all types of occasions. They have always been a symbol of love. It can be free or expensive. In your relationship, a gift means so much more. If the language of love is present, the most important thing to remember is them. It shows that you are thinking of them.

One of the most powerful gifts is when there is a crisis. Being there for them shows you care and are in tune with their needs. You are not giving a physical gift; you are giving yourself as a gift. The next best gift will be the gift from your heart. These gifts are those you make or do for your spouse to show how much they mean to you. They do not need money. They need your time to make your gift special. The best example is when a child makes a homemade Mother's Day card and a flower out of paper. They may even draw a picture. These are the types of gifts that are the most meaningful.

Now that you have an idea of each love language turn to <u>Appendix B</u> and take the survey. This will help you to determine which love language you are. Have your spouse take it as well, and you must be aware of each other's language. You no longer need to be speaking different languages inside your marriage.

There are three requirements for having an amazing intimate relationship. They are simple. Each one of these aspects can fall into one of these areas. I call it *"the triangle of Love."*

Passion or the Physical Side of the Triangle

In a relationship, we need three things to make it last. The first of these is physical. Our passion is what drives us. Pushing us towards romance and spicing up our marriages. It is the desire of love that guides us through our physical attraction for our spouse.

Intimacy or the Emotional Side of the Triangle

Intimacy is not all about sex. It is about going to the deeps of the abyss and sharing your deepest secrets. You know the heart of your spouse. You have adventured into this abyss together to explore and enjoy the journey. You fight through temptations together. You know and understand the deepest secrets of your partner. Love will not and cannot survive without Intimacy.

Commitment or the Cognitive Side and is the Base of Our Triangle

When you are married, you committed to each other. You are willing to travel the world together. You face challenges as a team. You are always there for each other. It is no wonder commitment is the base of our triangle. Your marriage will not last if you do not commit to each other.

Each of these sections will be combined to form a triangle. This intimacy triangle is needed as you and your spouse take this big adventure together. Find your love language and start speaking to one another in the same style of love.

Chapter 8: Tips for Strengthening Your Relationship

There are so many ways to strengthen your Marriage. A healthy marriage makes a strong family. Try some of these different ideas in your relationship and watch your relationship grow more durable and more reliable over the years. Pick your favorite plans and make them a routine for you and your spouse.

Couples Planning

We all get busy. Sometimes you need to schedule activities or set reminders. Getting together with your spouse to plan for the upcoming week is a great way to ensure everyone's needs are there to open the lines of communication in your relationship.

Think about the different activities you want to do together throughout the week. What will you do for date night? What will you have for dinner each night? These types of questions are a must.

Now it is your turn. Put this book down, sit down with your spouse, and start making a list of questions, activities, etc. that you want to discuss in each session. You should do this as a couple. Make sure you schedule a time for the two of you. Having a plan is very important. It will not only draw you closer as a couple, but it will also help you save money, which is fulfilling one of the top 5 for her.

Set Goals

Setting goals is a great way to keep your focus. During your couple's planning, you should set goals together. You should both agree with the objectives. Set them for six months. During each planning session, look at how you did with your goals and assess your progress. Keep a record of your goals and post them where both of you look daily. Most of the time, this is on the refrigerator.

The quest is, *"What should the goals be?"* There are seven areas I want you to focus on thinking, and I want you to write seven different goals. That would be one goal for each area. They are:

- Social
- Spiritual
- Family
- Health
- Intellectual
- Financial
- Career

Each of these areas of focus is to address the top 5 of men and women. Along with your 6-month goal, make short goals that you do each week to accomplish the goal in six months to help you focus more on your spouse's needs. At the end of the 6-months, assess the results for the next set of goals for the next six months.

Make a Budget

Preferably one of you makes the budget, or you work together on it; you both need to know it and follow it. I highly recommend you work together on making the budget. Working together will help strengthen your Marriage. To maintain a successful budget, you must work together. You are a team. Therefore, you must both agree on the budget.

You should have an area set aside for couple and family activities. You already know what you are planning for through your panning sessions, let your budget fit those needs. At first, you may not think a budget is essential. Maybe you will say, *"My spouse takes care of the finances; so, we are good."* The fact is, working together will bring your relationship to a new level. It will strengthen you as a team.

It is easy to spend money. I love to spend money while my wife would instead save it. It balances itself out. That is why I let her take care of all the finances. Granted, we still need a budget. A budget helps us to stay focused on what is important and to not spend money on things we do not need or is unimportant. When we both know what is in the budget, I am more likely to not spend the extra money. You never know what may come up. If we did not have a budget, there would not be any savings for a rainy day.

Time for an *"Hour of Honesty"*

Marriage can be a challenge. There will be things that bother you about your spouse. The first reaction is to react. That means you get irritated or upset. Most of the time, these emotions are over small things that do not matter. Do not try to change your partner. Instead, set some time each week to have an *"Hour of Honesty."* Being honest with each other is a must. You should always be an open book to your partner. If setting aside one hour a week is too hard, try one hour a month and work your way to having it weekly.

You are probably saying, *"I am already honest with my partner; why do I need an hour of honesty?"* That is awesome if you are already honest with your spouse. Granted, having an hour of honesty is different than being honest with your spouse. During this hour, you sit down together and talk about what has bothered you about the other person. You must agree that there will be no grudges, and you will not be offended by what the other person says. This is your chance to be heard by your spouse. This will strengthen your relationship by allowing each partner to feel they have been heard by the other.

There are two fundamental aspects to the *"Hour of Honesty."* You must SPEAK what is on your mind, and, LISTEN intently without interrupting the other person. LISTENING and SPEAKING are the keys to effective communication.

Date Night

For most of us, leaving your children is hard. You are used to doing everything as a family. However, you must make time for each other. Set a date night. This can be anything you want to do as a couple. If you cannot leave your kids, wait until they go to bed, cuddle up in front of the television with some popcorn and a drink, and watch a movie. You could even go hiking or dinner together.

The point of date night is for you to have some alone time together. Make it a goal to do this once a week if you can. Having that time together will help strengthen your relationship. If you need to, put it on the calendar and schedule date night. This ensures nothing will interfere with this great night of romance, passion, and togetherness. You will find yourself falling in love all over again as you remember why you fell in love, to begin with.

Always have a babysitter on call. My wife and I enjoy going out to dinner. We love Chinese food. When the babysitter arrives, we will go out for dinner. Even if it is only for a short time, this allows us to get closer and enjoy each other's company. Sometimes, we may go for a long drive in the mountains and enjoy nature. It may not seem like much; however, spending time together means the world.

Let's Be Intimate

Being intimate with your spouse is a vital component of a fantastic relationship. Keep in mind, intimate is not just about sex. Intimate with your spouse is not only measured in hugging, touching, and kissing. It is also about looking into each other's eyes and admiring the person you fell in love with. It is about holding hands and talking to each other at night in bed before going to sleep, and without electronics like a television or mobile phones. It is about cuddling with each other and enjoying the companionship of your partner. Most importantly, it is about bringing your relationship to a higher emotional level.

You are together for a reason. Enjoy the company of your spouse. Before you go to bed, you should enjoy their company by being with them.

Family Night

For those who have children, having a family night is as essential as a date night. This is your date night as a family. Find something you enjoy doing as a family. Try to have a family night once a week. Be sure to schedule it into the calendar. This will allow your family to be healthier; however, it will strengthen your relationship with your spouse as parents of these beautiful children.

In our family, we enjoy our family time. We play a lot of games. Sometimes, we get so busy that we schedule our family time to ensure everyone is available at that time. Some of the games we enjoy playing are dominoes, Monopoly, Charades, and checkers. Sometimes we also enjoy a fun ride as we sing to the radio. One of our favorite activities is karaoke night. We set up the microphones, turn on the television, and sing our hearts out. It is so much fun. There was one time that I was trying a fast song. The kids thought it was so funny that I was out of breath, trying to keep up with the words. It is essential to share in a good laugh. Even if it is at the expense of dad.

The family night should be full of fun and excitement. It gives everyone something to look forward to and bond together as a family.

Technology Free at Night

There is a severe problem in most relationships. All of us have mobile phones, iPads, tablets, televisions, and other electronics. These are a significant distraction in a relationship. Today, people cannot put them down. Their whole lives are on electronic devices. I am not saying never use them. Throughout the day, it is nice to have these devices. However, at night, when you are with your family and spouse, you should put them away. We can refer to this as *"Unplugging yourself."*

How can you spend quality time with your spouse if you have a mobile phone in your hand? Put it away at night. Turn off the television and spend time enjoying each other. I want you to take it to the next step, turn off your mobile phone or leave it in another room.

For example, I have a friend who has an elderly mother. It is essential to have the phone left on. However, for him to unplug himself, he leaves the ringer on high with it set on a table outside of the bedroom. This will allow him to get to it in a hurry if there is an emergency; yet, it allows him to enjoy the company of his wife.

As you *"unplug yourself"* from the world of technology, you will begin to see your relationship find that higher level of emotional connection. Watch your relationship grow and thrive.

Leave the Argument Until Sunday

In every relationship, there will be arguing. If someone says, *"We never argue or have a disagreement,"* then that couple is not being honest with you or themselves. It happens; especially, in the early stages of your marriage. Therefore, I want to introduce a technique that will help. This technique is, *"Leave it Until Sunday."*

Through this technique, you will get a clearer understanding of the arguments that really matter. When you have an argument that cannot be solved, put it to the side and wait until Sunday. Letting the argument set through the week, you may realize that it was not significant. However, you can sit down together on Sunday and discuss what you were arguing about. Although, if it is not an issue after that time, do not bring it back up. Forget about it and move on or talk about it and move on. If it is easily forgotten, then the argument did not matter.

The thing you do not want to find yourself doing is forgetting the fundamental issues. You will want to work through them. Anything that is a significant impact on your relationship and family must be discussed. From my experience, if there is an argument, most of the time, it is never vital. The major issues will not cause an argument.

When my spouse and I argue, it is always about little things that are not important. We have found that when we argue, 100% of the time, we do not remember what the argument is about the next day. The reason is the argument was not necessary. The things we remember are what we do together as a couple and a family. Those are the essential things. We also recognize the times we talk about important issues. The critical problems never cause an argument.

Never Go to Bed Mad

If you have been married more than a day, you have heard the saying, *"never go to bed mad."* This saying is genuine. Granted, we just got through talking about *"Leaving it Until Sunday."* It is still possible to never go to bed mad. With this technique, you have both agreed on the terms and are okay with them. That means you should not be going to bed angry as you are leaving those issues behind you until Sunday.

How can you talk or enjoy each other if you are mad? It is impossible to grow your relationship if you are angry at bedtime. You will dwell on the issue, and it will affect your time together and your sleep. You will not get good sleep, which will affect your job. Then it will affect your finances and the needs of your spouse. As it concerns the needs of your spouse, it will diminish the strength of your relationship due to their needs not being met. All this from going to bed mad.

Resolve the significant issues before bed and agree to leave the minor problems until Sunday while you move on from it. If you have questions at bedtime, talk about them without arguing and resolve the issue. If it is on your mind when you go to bed, it must be severe enough that you should take care of it immediately.

Trust Falls

For years, trust falls have been used in businesses as a team-building activity. You stand in front of your co-worker with your back towards them. Then you fall backward and trust that they will catch you. It gives you a sense of trust for your co-workers. It is the same with your spouse.

I know it sounds funny. You should trust each other. Maybe you are asking, *"We already trust each other, why do we need to do a trust fall?"* Trust falls are a way to confirm that you trust each other completely. You need to know if your partner will be there for you are if you will fall to the floor. Even if you say you trust your partner, this trust will help you to commit to the other openly fully.

On occasion, my spouse and I will be in the store, and she leans towards me. She fully expects me not to let her hit the floor. It is unexpected. When she does it, she has confirmation that I will always be there by her side. I am always there to catch her.

Activities List of Fun

There should be fun and excitement in your relationship. As a couple, start making a list of activities you would like to do as a couple and a family. Keep in mind, you should not combine your family activities with your activities as a couple. Keep them separate. Even if you have children, you still need that time as a couple. This can be as easy as going to the local museum or a Caribbean Cruise together.

To get you to start, here are, a few suggestions for your couples list:

  - Museum

- ➢ Cruise
- ➢ Hiking
- ➢ Camping
- ➢ Road Trips
- ➢ Weekend Vacations
- ➢ Date Night
- ➢ Drive through the Countryside
- ➢ Going to the Gym as a Couple

Your children and family are essential. We also need a list of your family activities. Here are a few suggests for your family list:

- ➢ Hiking
- ➢ Camping
- ➢ Fishing
- ➢ Museum
- ➢ Family Trip
- ➢ Family Movie Night
- ➢ Family Game Night
- ➢ Making S'mores (kids love Smores)

You can add these to your list if they fit into your interests. However, I want you to stop reading and start making your list. Think of what you like to do as a couple and what your family likes to do. This will give you a great resource as you plan your family and date nights.

This quality time is essential to the health and strength of your relationship. Use these lists as a guide. Let your children help with the family list as you work with your spouse on the couples list.

An Appreciation List

So many couples feel they are in a one-sided relationship. These feelings come from the feeling of not being appreciated. How many times do you tell your spouse that you understand and appreciate them? Perhaps, you feel like you do not need to say it to them. You think, *"They already know how much you cherish them."* The truth is, maybe they do not know your appreciation. They may need to hear it once in a while.

This is a great way to show your appreciation for your partner. Make a list of all the things you appreciate about your spouse. Do not stop adding to the list. You can start with the most common situations. At the end of the week, add everything you were appreciative of your spouse for that week. Share your list with your spouse and put your list where they can see it. Give them something to look forward to each week as you update it.

To get you started with your list, here are a few ideas:

> Cooking Dinner
> Washing Clothes
> Cleaning the House
> Providing for the Family (financially)
> Supporting Each Other
> Taking care of the children
> Etc.

This list is only to get you started. Think about all the things your spouse does daily. By showing your appreciation for your spouse, it will help strengthen your relationship and remind them how important they are to your life.

Compliment Jar

You now have a great start to your appreciation list. I want you to take your appreciation for each other to the next level. Start creating a compliment jar. This works with your appreciation list. Take each item on the list and put each one on small strips of paper. Put each strip of paper into a jar. Each day, before you start your day, take out a piece of paper. This will act as a constant reminder of how appreciated you are by your spouse. This will be a great way to rekindle your marriage or strengthen it. Bring back your appreciation for each other and watch how your relationship grows.

Encouragement Lists

Everyone needs encouragement. Think about ways your spouse can encourage you. Make a list of about ten things. Exchange your lists. Be sure to follow what is on the list consistently.

I have been writing for a long time. However, I always doubted my abilities. I stopped writing, even though it was my passion. I did not dare to write for others. I always felt my writing was not good enough. I did not know what to expect from others if they would read my work. My fear came from my thoughts of people not liking my writings. My wife saw me having doubts about myself, and she told me, *"you never know until you try it."* My wife told me to believe in myself. If you never believe in yourself, how can you expect others to believe in you? Through her encouragement, I was able to pursue my abilities to write.

Encouraging each other shows your partner how much you believe in them. Be their number one fan and be the cheerleader to their success. Let them know whatever their success or failures are; they are not alone. You are always by their side. Having that encouragement and support will make all the difference in your future and your relationship.

Question Jar

When I was in school, on the first day of school, the teacher had this unique way of introducing yourself. They would have a question jar. The task was to stand in front of the class and give your name, age, and so on. After the necessary information, you would pull out a question from the jar and answer what is on the piece of paper. These questions were designed for your teacher and classmates to know more about you.

The same concept can be used in your relationship. Set down as a couple and have fun making questions for the jar. If you have children, involve them in the activity. Do not answer the questions when you create them. Now you have your jar full of questions. Each day take one of the questions out of the jar and answer it. This activity is a great way to know more about each other.

To get you started, here are a few questions:

- What is your favorite car?
- Where did you go to school?
- What was your favorite class in school?
- As a child, what did you want to be when you grow up?
- What are your favorite hobbies?
- What was your most memorable family trip?

You should fill up the jar with questions. You could take each question to your spouse and answer it, or you can take it a little further and be creative in your answer. The best way to improve your relationship is through your creativity. For example, for you wanted to be a writer when you grow up, you can write a story for your spouse with the focus on the question and the answer in the story. Have fun with it. Be sure to have the question within your response so that your spouse knows it is the answer to your question. The time you spend on the answer through your creativity will show them how much they mean to you.

Exercise Together

It is essential to stay healthy. You should work on keeping your marriage and body healthy and active. A great way to help not getting bored during your relationship is through exercising and staying fit together. This gives you both the mindset of wellbeing. Your relationship needs to stay healthy.

As an example, my wife loves to exercise. She wants a more active lifestyle. She is always on the go. One day, she convinced me to join her morning exercises. The next thing I know, exercising together is part of my morning routine. I now realize it can be fun, exciting, and challenging. Now my spouse and I have an exercise goal. Our goal is to be healthier and lose a little weight. Working out together helps us to motivate each other. We do things like walking on the treadmill and jumping rope together. Along with our health, it gives us a chance to talk and interact with each other.

Make Healthy Friendships with Other Couples

Your best friend should be your spouse. However, it is nice to have other friends. The friends you make should be other couples who have healthy relationships. Relationships are contagious. If your friends have a broken relationship, eventually, you may catch it; however, if they have a healthy relationship, you may pick that up as well. That is why it is so important to have friends who have a healthy relationship.

I want to give you a caution. Do not make friends with singles, especially if they are of the opposite sex. That could destroy your marriage faster than having friends with a broken relationship. Always make friends as a couple. You want to strengthen your relationship. It is said, *"the strength of your relationship can be determined by the friends you keep."*

The Strength of Your Relationship Can be Determined by the Friends You Keep.

Entertain Your Friends

Some couples may not be into pleasing others. They may not even have friends at their homes. However, it gives your relationship a sense of being unified. You must work together to have a great party or entertain your friends. Therefore, as you have people over, you learn to have teamwork.

Volunteer Together

What do you believe? What is your mutual interest? As a couple, find something you both feel that you are okay working as a team and will grow from it. Give yourself to that cause. It does not matter if you help at an elderly home or through your church. Whether you involve yourself and your spouse to join a cleanup project in your community, do it as a couple and volunteer. One way you discover your shared values is through energetic bonding exercise. Looking for the best volunteer program for you as a couple requires more discussion, sharing opinions, and knowing each other's passion is what matters most. Doing activities like these will help you have a sense of service to others and make you feel good and proud of yourself. It will brighten your marriage and motivates you more. Take it the next step to strengthen your family when you involve your children as well.

This is a small list of suggestions for your marriage. Each one can bring something different into the relationship. Use them to help create an unbreakable chain between you and your spouse. As you think of new ways, add them to this list and watch your relationship with your spouse and family flourish.

Chapter 9: Main Reasons for Divorce

Research says an absence of commitment causes the most common reasons for divorces, too much fighting, marrying young and lack of preparation, not financially ready, having different religious beliefs and cheating.

Divorce is hard on a family. It will shatter all the dreams that you once build in your marriage. Imagine what it does to the children and how it could affect their lives. They begin to feel like the divorce is their fault. It does not matter what their ages are. They will all feel the same emotions. They will never fully understand. When they get older, it still bothers them, and they start to feel resentment against one parent or both. Sometimes, even to the point of hating you. The time when parents move on to live separate lives, the children are emotionally broken.

Before I met my wife, I went through a divorce. I had children with my previous spouse. They were still young at that time. Yet, as they got older, they developed hatred towards me. It has gotten to the point that they will not even talk to me. Each experience is different for parents and children, while, in my case, they hate me. As a parent, it does not matter how they feel about you, and you still love them.

Throughout history, divorce traces back to ancient times. Each married individual tends to terminate the union due to some aspects affecting their marriage life. Today, in most countries, divorce is permitted to give a permanent solution instead of separation. This is due to the legal aspect.

Here are some of the most common signs and factors which lead to divorces. Through the acronym D I V O R C E., we see a clearer picture.

D – Denial

As a couple, you deny there is a marital problem, and you find it difficult to accept that you are having this experience. You refuse to believe your relationship is hurting, and you are trying to find ways to fix it. The first stage is when your partner does not treat a serious problem that starts to cause a detachment. It could be in the form of finances, emotional needs, and intimacy. It must be dealt with immediately and not cause further damage.

You need to be sensitive to each other's needs. We have heard couples always say they are fine, but inside their home, there is a different atmosphere. They are refusing to accept the truth about something not right, and it is driving a wedge between them. They always pretend to be okay, so it will reduce stress and attempt to have confrontation avoidance. Each partner avoids talking about the issue, or they do not acknowledge the advice and concern of their spouse.

Remember, it is always healthy for a couple to engage in serious talks. When we effectively talk about our trials, hardships and temptations will result in drawing us closer and tightening the bonds of your relationship. Usually, in the denial state, a person may blame the other and not acknowledge their participation at all. Sometimes in an extreme case, this may lead to substance abuse as an escape to the reality in their marriage.

Honesty has a crucial role in the battle of denial. Both of you need to know that they are imperfect; thus, they need each other's gentle reproach. When you begin to be honest, your partner will see a genuine response to their needs and wants. It will lead to openness instead of criticism. I often tell my deepest secrets and fantasies to my wife just to know where she comes into my life. Likewise, she'll be honest about what she needs and expects from me. Honesty resolves our issues, and we both feel that our needs are met.

I – Interest for Others

One of the biggest killers in a relationship is when you start to develop feelings for someone who is not your spouse. You will tear down their trust, hope, dreams, and respect. You will be the cause of their low self-esteem, self-worth, and severe depression. It is a breaking of the commitment you made to each other through emotional and physical aspects.

You need to be happy and satisfied with who you are married to. You married the one who you love for a reason. Hold onto that reason for the rest of your life. Even thought of someone else in a romantic way will lead to the desire to be with them. It must be stopped before it starts. If you genuinely love your spouse, those thoughts will not be there.

Extramarital affairs often start with wishing, wanting, and desiring others. Some people cheat to keep away from being bored. Many times, they feel they do not get respect from their partner, and they are looking for someone who has that missing factor. Sometimes people cheat because they have the chance to do it. All these things may lead to divorce. However, this does not always end up that way; sometimes, a couple may find they are more durable after recovering on the partner's infidelity.

The truth is, running away from any form of temptation is always the best option. God did not assure us we would never be tempted, but when the time comes, he will come up with an escape. Once broken, it's always hard to repair the trust that you once had. These affairs will lead to deterioration of confidence in your marriage and of each other. There are sayings, *"a cheater is always a cheater"* and *"once popped you can't stop."* Even though these statements hold in many situations, it does not mean that person cannot stop and change their life around. Remind them of how much you care for them and help them through it.

When a marriage survives a catastrophe like this, it will take years to rebuild what you once had. The truth is, some couples survived this ordeal, and I admire how they remain faithful after the incident.

As the married couple takes this journey, they invite the thrill and magic of their passion for slowly decreasing over time. Thus, thrill-seeking with others remains a constant threat to Marriage. As you go back to the basics, communicate in full honesty. There is nobody who can understand your fantasies and desires aside from your lifelong partner. Remember, you are a team. A change in perspective can help you better understand each other and work toward a solution to your problem. There is a solution to everything.

V – Vices

Having vices in your relationship can lead to a devastating marriage. I am talking about all unhealthy addictions to include social media, food, alcohol, drugs, shopping, pornography, or gambling that could negatively affect the marriage life. These addictions may replace your time with your spouse, and it becomes the third party in your relationship. Instead of being interested in others, you are interested in your vices. The results are the same.

You may seem helpless battling addictions that may require specific medical interventions such as therapy and counseling. When you spend too much time on gadgets and technologies that diminish your quality time with your partner, you have created an unhealthy vice that is affecting your relationship in a negative way.

In my years of Marriage, our bedroom becomes a no gadget zone. We unplug for the night. We focus on our partner, and communication becomes more transparent and better without the annoyance of the internet craze. Sex becomes more intimate.

We set our limitations on the credit cards and never buy what is not on our purchase list unless it is for emergency reasons. We share passwords and logins to check each other's financial health, emails, etc. Thus, creating our relationship as an open book to each other.

Gambling and other food, alcohol, and drug addictions require more professional help. Your support and encouragement are crucial to their outcome and success. It involves patience and persistence until your spouse is free from any addiction. It is gratifying when your partner overcomes these obstacles, and you did it together. You are a team. When one partner has an issue to work through, you both have the same problem and need to work through it together. It is hard to do it on your own.

O – Overfamiliarity

There is a famous saying, *"familiarity breeds contempt."* Overfamiliarity happens when you know so much of your spouse that it causes you to disrespect your partner along the way, which results in yelling, criticism, complaining, and the list goes on and on. These are the results of seeing all the bad qualities and actions. You know your spouse so well that you anticipate their reactions, and you already know what their opinion will be based on the topics you talk about. Years of being together can cause you to take them for granted or help you to appreciate them more.

Having Contempt in your marriage will constitute a lack of respect for your partner's ability. Thinking you are better than your partner can always lead to a heated argument. The big question is, *"What is the antidote?"* The answer is easy. Never stop learning new things from your partner. It's called curiosity.

The magic begins when the unfamiliar becomes familiar as you discover each other and start to let go of your previous judgments and opinions. You begin to like and dislike the same things.

When my wife and I first met, we had different tastes in food. I enjoy Italian and Mexican food; whereas, she enjoyed Asian food. As time goes by, we experience the choices of food each of us likes. We became familiarized with the foods we love. Now my wife and I enjoy the combination of all three.

The eagerness and legitimate interest are essential as you get to know more about your spouse and their abilities to create more significant opportunities for you to experience delight and enjoyment in your relationship. That's why I never stop believing in my wife. I involved her so much on all our decisions because I think two heads are better than one. The more my wife and I interact with specific topics, the more we come up with an agreeable solution. Familiarity in marriage gives me a chance to discover the way my wife thinks, and she knows what I am thinking. Most of the time, I find it amusing that her options are far better than mine, and we had the same idea only it was worded differently.

R – Resentment

Resentment usually happens when married couples have their fairy tale expectations and end up being bitterly disappointed. Most of them believe in the famous line, *"they lived happily ever after."* The truth is, this only happens in fairytales and not in real life. However, you can create a "happy ever after marriage" together.

Resentment results from unhealthy patterns and poor habitual behaviors of your partners. In general, your marriage will have ups and downs. It is the negative attitude towards your partner, which leads to the buildup of resentment.

In my previous marriage, I would go to work, clean the house, cook, and take care of the children. I developed resentment towards her because I felt she was not doing her part. All she did all day was spending time on the computer talking to other people. She took me for granted. I could not say anything at first because she would get mad. I was so frustrated that I would unplug the internet, which leads to a heated argument. The resentment I had for her slowly got worse and added to the reasons for divorce.

Resentment builds in Marriage when thrills shifted from focus, time, and effort on each other and redirected to your job, children, or other selfish behaviors. They thought that these pleasures during courtships would extend their marriage life. It may sound absurd, but you should never forget to add spices and thrills even you are married.

Remember, resentment can build upon particular simple neglect of daily chores or assignment to more complicated issues like failing to celebrate your anniversary or any specific date. At first, you won't know if your spouse is resenting you, but sooner or later, you will notice it when the coldness begins to engulf the relationship. There will be a constant tension between you, and it will create holes in your relationship, which will cause your marriage to be at risk and slowly begins to fade away.

Be sensitive to your spouse's feelings and offer a solution through compromising with a sincere heart to heart talk. You need to meet each other halfway by sharing your answers and listening to what they say. Talk with your partner and discuss what halfway means. Remember, you are a team in everything you do.

When I became too much of a workaholic, then my wife suggested leaving all my job-related concerns and work at the office. When at home, I should focus on the family. It took a lot of effort on my end, but eventually, this started to work for us. It took a lot of courage and practice for us to be vocal about our ill-feeling towards each other. When we would express our feeling, we forget the value of the tone in our voices. Resentment can be created through the way we say things and not only the words we use.

Early in our marriage, I would spend a lot of time doing work. I would go to work for eight hours and then bring unfinished work home so that it is done for the next day. My wife noticed and started to resent me for being a workaholic. She eventually mentioned what she noticed. I could see the resentment that was created by my work, and the tone created more resentment.

C – Complacency

Complacency in marriage happens when some couples are so using to each other that every day is the same. There is no excitement in the relationship. You get to apply to each other. Troubles tend to arise when you become complacent, and you start to drift apart until it is too late to fix.

Being extremely comfortable with your partner can lead you to complacency. This kind of contentment in a marriage can lead your relationship to apathy, hostility, and indifference. It's like cancer that eating your flesh slowly until you no longer can prevent further damages. The chances of being cured for cancer are at best during early detection. That is why so many divorces happen in the later years of marriage, causing the thrill and magic to decrease.

Every relationship needs a boost of excitement. Marriages breakdown because of a lack of desire and passion. That's why you need to be mysterious again. It may sound silly, but you need your spouse to go, *"Huh?"* or say, *"I never thought you could do that."* Let your spouse hear *"wow"* and the *"oh"* again. Always keep the mystery alive and find yourself being unpredictable. Rekindle your marriage and bring the thrill and excitement back. As you do, your relationship will begin to flourish again; you will start to remember why you were married.

E – Equality

Equality in a relationship means you both respect each person's interests and desires without the biased through gender or status. If you marry someone with a strong personality, the need of submission is extreme. Sometimes you give up on your interest to avoid a heated argument. This type of relationship is based on power and control instead of equality and respect, which leads to turmoil. When it is left unchecked, it will lead to more resentment and bitterness.

For example, I love going out and taking videos and pictures with my drone. My wife loves Korean dramas. We respect the interest of the other person. We each have our likes and dislikes, even though we are individuals with different cultures. We are equals in the relationship. I am not biased towards different cultures, and she is okay with the things I like.

Remember, love gives us the freedom to choose and not be selfish, which everything is centered on you. Learn to always involve your spouse in all decisions and choices to avoid the blaming game. You can enjoy mutual accomplishments when the end leads to your success as a couple. Celebrating the outcome and having an enjoyable moment.

Healthy relationships are based on mutual respect and know how to compromise. Resolving conflicts in a right way is needed. It is okay to disagree sometimes, but you need to work on a solution that is acceptable to both partners without arguing or getting physical. Sometimes you both must agree and disagree with solving the problem.

In compromising, you need to be honest about your feels and sometimes telling your spouse what you feel. With gentle changes to your partner's decision will lead to a more balanced relationship. Honest communication is always the key.

Chapter 10: Dealing with Temptations

Every day we are faced with temptations. They can be anything from getting a new motorcycle to cheating. Anytime we are tempted to do something we know, we should not do it is a temptation.

For me, my biggest temptation is chocolate. Even though chocolate is not a serious offense in a marriage. Yet, it is still a temptation. The problem is, the way we deal with our temptations. If you have a chocolate temptation, let your spouse help you kick it. They will gladly hide it from you, so you cannot find it.

I remembered a few years ago, and I was craving chocolate. My wife does not allow me to have much, and so the craving is always here. I went to the store to get groceries and picked up some chocolate. I snuck it home and hid it under the bed. Little did I know she was cleaning the bedroom that day. The chocolate that was hiding was found. What a sad and depressing day. Chocolate is one thing, but what about temptations in your marriage? There are some severe temptations that you must avoid. I realize that you cannot stop your urge of attractions. The best solution is to run away.

The history of temptation goes back during pre-historic times. It is as old as, back to the Garden of Eden. The devil, in the form of a serpent, tempted the first humans, Adam and Eve. They fell for the lies the serpent told them. The Bible says a lot of stories about the temptation. It has always been a part of human nature to be tempted. Temptations are brought our curiosity; we indulge in things that entice us, gratify us, and makes us feel emotions we have not thought for a long time. Temptations come in several different ways, such as eating healthy foods, maintaining a good lifestyle, managing finances, and attraction to someone. There is a lot of ways to be tempted. In some context, the temptation is connected to sin for those who sinned are those that cannot resist temptation. The temptation may be used to the state of being satisfied without following moral standards.

The attraction is one way to be tempted, and perhaps the reason is why affairs and sexual intimacy to someone other than your partner are happening. Although it is reasonable to be attracted to other people, what matters is how you act on those feelings and how you stop it before it creates sin in the marriage.

In marriage, every affair begins with a temptation of an attraction. Marriages break up because one partner loses themselves in fascination and thinks they can get away with it. One selfish act can wipe out your relationship and vanish the years of integrity. Most families are broken caused by one of the parents having an affair and not thinking about what effects it may have.

In some cases, the notion of a marital affair will always lead to blaming the husband. In every cheating husband, there must also be a cheating woman.

Extramarital relations outside marriage where an illicit romance or sexual relationship, romantic friendship or intimate attachment occurs are being done by two persons. An affair that continues in one form or another for years will eventually lead to separation and divorce.

In a marriage concept, temptation often builds up when one partner started looking for someone who treats them better than their spouse. A marriage becomes weak when facing problems; for example, a wife becomes attracted to a man who empathizes and listens to her more. Both partners are susceptible to committing a mistake. Marital problems were existing between partners, and it has become easy to look for others who will give them the attention they are not getting from their spouse. It is a human weakness to fall for someone who gives them more attention and affection. Eventually, confiding their problems to that person will lead to closeness resulting in an affair.

The temptation is one of the challenges married couples are facing. Together, we will learn how to identify various ways on how to deal with temptation. You will learn the underlying factors that cause temptation to exist in your marriage and its consequences if it continues to exist. Each topic will provide you with solutions that refrain you from being tempted. However, this will only serve as a guide for married couples that are currently facing temptation as a challenge but not to the extent that would provide an exact solution to the matters at hand. Spouses need to keep an open mind when working out a marriage, it is not suitable for judging your spouse if they committed a mistake, but rather it will be helpful if you keep an open ear and trust them to be honest about their confession. Marriage is hard work, and making it successful takes a lifetime. It is only common for couples to experience temptation along the way; the important thing is to have both partners to be determined to drive against it.

Take the time to go over the list of ways on how to battle temptation. It will provide insights that can assist couples in determining ideas on how to overcome temptation. It is better to discuss this with your partner to be able to come up with a solution that could help you resolve your situation.

The Courage to Resist Temptation

Temptation can be described as an immediate pleasurable urge and impulse to fill the void of something lacking. It exists because something is lacking in a married couple's life. Some say affairs happen because the love of each spouse was no longer alive. It Involves a romance that brings back those memories of being pursued, excitement, and sexually intimate. It makes you feel young and being wanted again.

One way to avoid temptation is to fill the void of whatever you feel is lacking in your relationship. Sometimes we compare our married life to others, and nowadays, with the use of technology, we often see the gaps in our relationship.

We long for consistency of love, touch, romance, and the desire brought about by our insecurities, making ourselves more vulnerable to temptations. We try to think of scenarios of *"what ifs."* What if our husband is more compassionate than he is now, practices romance, and remembers all the special occasion? Then maybe we wouldn't be tempted to look for others in the first place. You try to picture a different person out of your husband throughout your marriage. You no longer admire the one you signed up for through marriage. We often believe that it is our husband's fault that you came looking for others, but it's not. Signing up for marriage is nothing like a membership club; you pay the fee and use it all you want. In marriage, you must make all the effort to keep your membership, or otherwise, you'll be taken out.

The critical thing to remember in resisting temptation is to have the *"courage"* to resist temptation. For instance, thinking of others through your thoughts during your marriage chaos, such as leaving your spouse or involving in an affair, will feel desirable at the moment; however, in the long run, it bears undesirable results. Exercising self-control is also essential; it makes us feel superior to our desires. Once we thought we are walking on the wrong path, we need to take a detour and regain control of ourselves. We need to paint the 'what will happen" if we succumb to temptation. Fixates ourselves to the aftereffects if we divulge on our selfish desires. We cannot sacrifice the well-being of our family. Giving in to temptation will result in a broken marriage and interfere with your long-term goals. We were making it easier to deal with temptation if you were avoiding what tempts you.

Do not Be Surprised When It Happens

Do not be afraid, but rather be prepared. Make it a habit dealing with temptation, for it's always there. Temptation can come in any form; for instance, your eating habits, sleeping routine, and managing your finances. Let us acknowledge that we will be tempted in all kinds somehow, but the upper hand of letting it happen is in our hands. You were born with the wisdom of differentiating what is wrong from right, and through this, we will be able to determine what is better.

You need to be prepared. Like commencing a *"fire drill"* in a school to make students and staff prepare in case, a real incident will happen. You need to equip yourselves with the knowledge that is beneficial for you in dealing with temptations. For example, exposing yourself to healthy foods through the process of not buying processed or carb-filled food will take you to your goals of achieving a healthy lifestyle. You need to have the determination to continue what you are starting.

Giving in to temptation is only one part of the journey, but do not be surprised if you find yourself on the verge of losing it. Be prepared and regain your self-control.

Ask for help

People with a strong sense of independence are not fond of asking for help in times of trouble. They believe it is their responsibility to resolve problems on their own without asking for help.

Most people think of a notion that temptation often leads to marital affairs. These stereotypes suppress people from talking about attractions. They don't want to be judged and make their family look as if they're breaking apart; therefore, keeping it from others. For some, the word temptation alone carries the burden history of a broken marriage and family. Most often, marital affairs are caused by temptation, such as husbands cheating on their wives or wives cheating on their husbands. The attraction had done its part in creating chaos in the married world.

It is good to be aware of another way of dealing with temptation is to ask for help. It is essential to have someone that you can consult with the same experiences you have. Knowing that someone has gone through what you are also going through is like a breath of fresh air. Through your friends, you can ask for help. For example, the way you resist temptation in a particular situation. It is always good to have someone who can understand where you are coming from and who will listen to your thoughts without judgment. Asking for help can have many benefits, such as helping you progress better and faster. Asking for help makes you feel more grateful, you develop your sense of trust, and strengthen your relationship to the people you confide in.

You are bound to live with companions, which is where the famous saying "No man is an island" comes from. Everybody needs a companion or friend. It is not a weakness to ask for help. If you choose to accept support from someone you can trust, they might teach you something new and provide you with more useful knowledge that you can use in your marriage.

Invest in Your Marriage

The media and technology influence our culture as it heightened our expectations in a relationship. We expect high levels of intimacy, communication, and personal fulfillment. With the perseverance and determination of each couple's relationship will flourish.

Make your marriage strong enough to combat temptation. Invest in your marriage by determining what is lacking in your relationship and discuss these over with your spouse. Be open about suggestions that could help you both. Most importantly, be honest with each other. Share your struggles; for example, you wanted to have more intimate date nights to rekindle romance or have more in-depth conversations that do not involve the kids or household. Be open about this struggle as this will acknowledge the flaws of your spouse and come up with solutions to resolve it.

You may devise a plan on how to manage your time to make up for the missed date nights or take a vacation without the kids. These *"date nights"* matter is due to the power they have in rekindling your relationship. They will lessen the chance for a marriage to end badly. Surprisingly, date nights have their advantages.

First, these date nights are an opportunity to communicate. They help deepen the understanding of one another and your relationship. It can improve how couples communicate as their relationship develops. You will experience new challenges and problems.

Second, they can strengthen a couple's commitment to each other, especially in times of trials, and overcome it with the help of strength brought about by date nights. Most significantly, a couple's time can minimize conflict and lessen the chance of divorce.

Set Boundaries

Establishing boundaries with your partner does not mean limiting their actions and happiness. There are misconceptions about putting up barriers in a relationship. You may feel these acts are no longer necessary for your partner. They should already know and act on your needs. Sometimes, they think these actions may ruin a relationship by invading their personal space and limiting their freedom. However, a healthy relationship cannot exist if these boundaries cannot be adequately communicated and are transparent. Setting boundaries may eliminate the chances of temptation.

Setting up boundaries could produce positive results if taken seriously. These boundaries will always serve as each other's reminder to be faithful and to avoid situations that could challenge your relationship. For example, as a married man, you are no longer able to be with other ladies whom your wife is not aware of; and as a wife, you cannot go to places with only a male companion.

These restrictions may be familiar to every married people, but if not taken earnestly, they can turn a marriage into a disaster, and temptation will come to a place. Setting boundaries and not executing them makes a person disrespectful and ruins some factors that bind a relationship together. If you respect this aspect, you can both feel safe and secure. Your marriage will grow, and your love for each other will shine through.

Boundaries do not always focus on the worse cases in a marriage. They can also refer to material things. For example, my wife and I know the binderies set in our marriage vows. We respect and honor them. However, we set other boundaries. I have a drone that she does not touch or fly without my permission. It is not because I do not trust her; although, she does not know how to operate it. She knows it means a lot to me. My wife respects my feels does not want to hurt me by ruining the drone. The same goes for her makeup. I do not touch her makeup for fear; I do not want to destroy it. Granted, I would look funny wearing her makeup anyways.

You must agree on the boundaries set in the relationship. In marriage, we agree on the vows or promises we make to each other. Set limits and follow them. These are ways of letting your spouse know you respect them and their desires.

Be open with your spouse

Open communication is one of the most important emotional needs that is essential for your marriage. Once you have fallen into temptation, it is necessary to tell your spouse and let them know what is going on with you without their knowledge. It is a normal reaction to feel attracted to the opposite sex, and it is standard to find some qualities in other people that your partner does not possess. When you start liking the other person, and if you feel it could create a misunderstanding between your spouse, then you must inform them, so they will help you carry the burden. Your spouse will help you to put the situation in check, so there's no hiding it that could ruin the trust. It is better not to wait until they find out about it, and they will think otherwise. It is one way of dealing with the consequences rather than keeping it from them. Hiding it inside may be what you would prefer to do since you do not want any confrontations, but it will put you in an unfavorable situation someday. That is why if you know your spouse will get upset, it means you should have known better than to behave that way in the relationship. You should take good care of your relationship with your spouse, it may not be perfect, but it is the right thing to do.

Taking into consideration the feelings of your spouse refrains you from committing a mistake. Hiding it promotes suspicion and doubts, and it could raise questions about honesty and trustworthiness in your marriage. It may not be easy to communicate with your partner about temptation. Frequently, they will misinterpret you. Other times, your partner will lessen their trust in you, but open communication creates an opportunity for both of you to build internal security within the family. Being transparent with one another means that you both are willing to see each other's worse, especially when you failed in some ways, and not being honest.

In our relationship, we try to be an open book. My wife and I are transparent with each other. We know everything that happens in and out of the relationship. If I need to leave the house, my spouse knows where I am going. She can call me at any moment to talk. Honesty is the best policy. We do not lie about where we are going or what we need to do. For example, when I have training for my job, I always tell her what happened during the training; considering, I am online at home. Therefore, I leave the office door open, so she knows what is happening.

Being transparent goes a lot further than just going out and what you are doing. She knows what the paycheck is each month. We do not buy anything without the other person knowing. That also goes to say; we do not buy anything without talking about it first. Regardless of who is making money, we both know what is in all bank accounts. That means, if we have personal accounts, we still know what is in these accounts. There are no secrets. Even with passwords and account information, we both know them. I use a program that is accessed on all computers and only accessed through the home to obtain our passwords. In that way, when a password is changed, everyone can see the new password.

Being open to your spouse is vital for the relationship. It shows trust and respect. Letting your spouse know you are doing what you said will strengthen the faith you have—creating a stronger bond between you.

Keep away from that individual

Distract yourself and keep away from that individual. One way of dealing with temptations is to avoid it and to stay out of it. Put your attention to something else rather than fixating your thoughts to something tempting you. Avoid the person you are attracted to or tempting you because constant contact would likely increase the pressure on continuing and wanting to do it.

For instance, if a co-worker likes you, you should tell that person that you are married, and you value your family. Make sure that person who was trying to tempt you knows that you are not interested in making any sort of relationship aside from your spouse. You must be transparent before anything leads in the wrong direction.

Lastly, do not engage in activities that involve your personal life, especially marital problems. Those activities can quickly turn into issues in your marriage. Affairs begin when people start talking about their pressures and challenges with another person other than their spouse. Then they feel that a person empathizes and understands them more than their partner. These could break the casualties between you two and lead into a feeling of closeness that left untreated will eventually lead to an affair.

Avoiding temptation is the best way not to sin against your partner. Keeping yourself in check with the consequences you may face will help you determine the right choices to make and put you in the right frame of mind. Remember, no temptation is little when your marriage is at stake that would eventually destroy everything. If it is a sin against your relationship, then it is not acceptable.

I had a friend in the military who had problems with a fellow soldier. He was a Noncommissioned Officer, and she was one of his soldiers. She enjoyed doing activities with him when they would go places. Keep in mind, and he is married. Eventually, he started to realize that she was developing feelings for him. He is always open with his spouse and let her know what was going on. He talked to his leader, and they moved her out of his leadership. This was to avoid any unfortunate situations. When he went out with his squad, it was always when she was not around. She was no longer under his leadership, which made it easier to do things with his team. He also informed his leader of the situation so they could be causes of it happening. This is a form of keeping away from the individual and still being transparent to your spouse.

When you are doing the right thing to avoid the situation, you will not have a wedge driven between you and your spouse. This is a sharp wedge that could send you into divorce. Do not allow it to happen. It is so easy to avoid the person. Walk away and never look back.

Remind Yourself of the Consequence

Giving in to temptation bears a lot of consequences, some of which may be fatal to your marriage and can result in a broken family. Others experience emotional impacts that negatively affect them, such as low self-esteem and insecurity. The person who got cheated on suffers a blow of low self-esteem, thinking there might be something wrong with them. They will believe that they are not good enough for the marriage since their partner is looking for the opposite of who they are. People who experience marital affairs have given up trusting people.

Next, you lose a sense of emotional stability. The temptation that leads to an affair makes you feel a lot of negative emotions such as frustrations, self-guilt, and anger, which, if combined, can turn into a mental breakdown and lead to depression. These are just some of the consequences a temptation that leads to an affair may bring. However, each sin carries with its negative after-effects; therefore, you must check yourself first before giving in to temptation.

There are many reasons for being tempted. Usually, this is without much thought and consideration of the effects it can have on the other person. These effects can be devastating and will cause a harmful impact and can take a long time before the person to heal from the effects it will cause.

Confide in your partner if something happens

You must tell your partner the truth before the situation gets worst. Being honest about it rather than keeping it from them could make the case more impactful. Honesty and trust are needed these circumstances, but if you explain it thoroughly and sincerely to them and admitting your faults may have a substantial impact in resolving the matter with minimum damage. After all, marriage is about accepting each other's faults and understanding them enough to forgive them for their bad choices.

You and your partner must be open to discussions about circumstances that are tempting you. You should be honest with each other and keep an open mind that your partner will not be likely to fall of temptation. Trust is there regarding opening topics that concern your loyalty. Thus, words and actions are essential to keep your partner suspecting. Prove to them you can handle resisting temptation without them worrying. These challenges will strengthen your marriage and maintains your loyalty to your union.

Confide in your partner when something happens, admit your faults, and ask for their forgiveness. Let them know everything about your situation, do not hide anything from them, and be sincere in confessing your thoughts and actions. Help them to understand where you are coming from and prevent them from feeling you are resentful. So long as you do not display ignorance when admitting your faults, you will be able to gain the trust of your partner again. It is possible to judge at first, but keep in mind that the normal reaction for sinning is to be upset.

Give the time your partner needs when processing their thoughts, be patient as possible, and never stops trying in asking for forgiveness. Nobody is perfect or has an excellent relationship. Everybody commits mistakes, yet, that is the reason forgiveness exists. Forgiveness is the anti-body of each poisoned relationship. Make your relationship affair-proof, provide the necessary treatment, and confiding in your partner whenever a bad situation happens or is about to happen. What a great way to make your relationship healthier.

Meet such persons in the open

When you meet people out in the open, you refrain from sharing intimate conversations or receiving personal interest from others, which could keep you from having an affair. Often, the feeling of closeness creates an advantageous atmosphere for the temptation to lurk on. Moreover, those married people with existing marital problems have become more vulnerable to temptation. If a person of the opposite sex comes along and provides comfort and care, they may pose as a better partner suited for them. People often fall for someone who cares and shows affection more than what they receive in their marriage. Letting these people in as a confidante in such a state of weakness will eventually fall into sin.

If someone is giving you more attention than what you are supposed to be getting, it is better to meet them out in the open with the company of friends instead of meeting them alone. This will make it so no intimate conversations will occur, and only casual conversation will happen between the two of you. It is better to bring friends at your own expense who are aware of your situation for they can provide an easy escape to avoid them. In terms of co-workers, it is better to limit your talk to casual conversation and only discuss matters relating to work. Have lunch together with the presence of co-workers and do not stay up late in the office with the person you are attracted to or vice versa. These are just one of the many ways to avoid temptation. For me, the best approach is to invite our spouse to these outings. What better way to avoid the temptation than having your true love there by your side?

Always be mindful that temptation exists in all things that you do; it's only up to you on how you are going to react. You are higher than each experience you take, and each circumstance turns out the way it does because you let it. You hold the upper hand.

Understanding these different ways of dealing with temptations can help couples in the battle. There is no perfect relationship, but there are stronger ones, which matters the most. Making your relationship durable will likely bring your marriage into success.

Chapter 11: Forgiveness

Getting hurt in a relationship is inevitable, things happened unexpectedly, and we tend to linger on those thoughts that caused us pain. Deep inside, we remember that there was a point in our marriage when our spouse intensely hurt and give us so much heartache.

To forgive someone is a choice, the more comfortable we forgive, the more lightness we feel in our hearts, and more positive thoughts we think. Holding on to anger is like a big rock that we carry inside and eats away our mental and emotional health. It will continue to eat at your relationship until there is nothing else to feed.

Forgiveness is not a privilege we gave to our partner; it is a choice that we made to ourselves to release the tension that we feel inside. Is forgiving a miraculous change? The answer is NO. It will not happen overnight. It is a state of mind that lets us diffuse whatever negativity grows inside us. Forgiveness is not for anyone but us, to protect our wellbeing and see life in a harmonious perspective.

Forgiveness in marriage allows you to think that we are not the victim forever; instead, it will give us the capability that you know how to move on and acknowledge the hurt and the pain caused by other partners. When you know how to forgive, you will see that you can leave negative emotions behind and ready to build a stronger bond with your spouse. Forgiveness will create more space in your heart and will wash away the mud that is residing there and disturbing your present moment.

Forgiving is the hardest thing in a relationship, but to what extent will you carry all these grudges and pain towards the other person by being so cold and distant? Ask yourself, *"is it worth it?"* The answer is, ABSOLUTELY YES. We are human; we made mistakes. Learn from them and move forward in your relationship.

When our spouse hurts us, we stop seeing all the goodness they have inside. We stop seeing that once not so long time ago, their presence was like oxygen that we breathed. We started to see them as the villain in the horror movies, and we begin to feel that we have to smash that monster that made our lives so miserable.   As we let our past affect us, we see nothing but the worst in our spouse's behavior. We forget their positive side as a person. It is easy for us to remember their wrong actions than speculate and retain their good deeds. It happens all the time, and it is happening everywhere.

In politics, one right running candidate can become a politician in no time. Still, one bad word or wrong advertisement in media can end his political career quickly. It is always easy for us to pinpoint the wrongs over what we do that is right in every situation.

An army veteran with an amputated arm; when he walks on the sidewalks, people would only look at his missing body structure but will not recognize his service to the country; to them, he will only be an amputee than a veteran.

It is in our nature to look for the errors in people faster than looking for what they have done right, our brain dictates it, and this is like forgiving someone who has caused us pain, one wrong action against us makes us hate that person a lifetime and forget everything they did. We judged them and found ways to punish and criticized them.

Forgiveness feels like it is impossible; especially, if it becomes a routine for that spouse to hurt you. Holding a grudge is much more comfortable, and it feels that you are getting even and taking an act of indirect revenge for not giving them a chance. In Marriage, forgiveness is part of the commitment you made to each other through vows of matrimony. You chose to accept the other for all the good and evil come what may. In marriage, we should practice forgiveness. Tell yourself that you need to forgive so you can move forward, or you will be stuck forever thinking about the person who hurt you. Bitterness in your marriage will eventually destroy you. It will results in changes in your physical well-being, causing irregular heart rate, higher blood pressure, and other harmful conditions. At the same time, forgiveness calms the mind and your inner self.

Marriage is like a newly opened gadget with assembly parts; we need to have all elements together to create the package and make it work. We cannot miss one piece if you want it to work correctly. It is the same in marriage. Every part has a place that makes up the whole thing to create a masterpiece between husband and wife. We can never become better at loving someone and give our whole self if we don't practice honesty, respect, and commitment. We can never become honest if we don't remember how to understand, and we can never know if we don't know how to forgive and let things go. Move on from the past hurt; we can never turn back times, what happens, happens.

Forgiveness is the key to open the door of a successful marriage. Forgiveness is a process and a procedure for the series of steps or actions taken to achieve a goal, it is a part of the process.

Here are some steps for this journey that could serve as a guide for you to make it through this part of your relationship.

Determine the Decision to Forgive

We can only let go of what kept us from forgiving if we find the courage *"to forgive."* To try is the very essence of striving. We will never know if we can forgive somebody if we do not work on trying. It is the start of the process. We have to start somehow, somewhere. No matter what our spouse had done to us, for us to keep our marriages floating, we need to take action to start forgiving. We can always ignore our spouse's faults. We cannot ever let them feel guilty about it all the time. It does not help anything; instead, it will fuel the fire that we already have inside.

We must come to the point that we need to do something about the problem, and deciding to forgive is a great place to start. We need to keep moving forward and determine the importance of forgiving our spouse. We need to see what lies behind this act and what we can gain from it. Maybe, if we decide to forgive, then we will change the way we are as a team. It will be beneficial for both of you and will significantly impact the importance of learnings along the way. We owe it to them as part of keeping our relationship together.

Remember that Forgiveness is a Process

We need to remember that forgiveness is a process, and everything takes time. Forgiveness is like water; before we can forgive, we need first to check that we have got hurt, and it takes a lot of time to heal so we can go back to the way things were before. We need to be patient and trust the timing of the healing process.

To forgive someone is not an easy task, but it takes a lot of courage and a rational mind to make your marriage work. If you want a long and lasting marriage wherein you are willing to see your spouse on their wrinkled and old days, then forgiveness is needed for your relationship to get through. Forgiving is the best time to think and look back to those times you once had. Having a passion for each other with the feel of being on top of the world. Remember, all the things your spouse did for you, and at one point in your marriage, you see your spouse as the best thing that ever happened to you.

Focus on what happens along the way and remember that it takes two to build or destroy a relationship. Check what went wrong and why the relationship went astray. This is the time to question yourself if the marriage is worth reconnecting again. Both partners are supposed to know how to accumulate problems. Criticizing your spouse for everything that happens in the past will eventually end up breaking the ties that bind, and divorce is the only option. You must keep in mind that forgiveness is one ingredient of a rewarding relationship.

Couples who forgive each other can clear out the awful hurt and resentment that holds them back so they can go back to the happy and exciting days. Couples need to feel connected to each other again and move on. They must forget the negative emotions that linger for them to create a healthier and happy married life.

Accept All Emotional Burdens

As human as we are, we all get stress emotionally due to unexpected reasons. This emotional stress sometimes happens when we are in the circumstances where we can not say no to a particular favor asked by others, but we have to do it for the sake of the person involved.

We need to accept all emotional burdens such as emotional and physical pain as part of the process and as part of our lives. If we felt sorrow as we undergo this journey, let it be. Feel the pain and learn from it. Let it hit us and acknowledge that it will always be there because, for us to move on to the other side of the bridge, we need to pass the bridge "itself." Cry if we need to, be weak, and then we will become stronger. Fall so you can get up for you to shine. Only if you confront your pain, you can challenge yourself, and you can start taking steps to move forward to a better you.

Search for a Brighter Ending

The only good thing that comes from a journey is the right destination. We need to remember the more important things that could happen if we look at the bright side. Search for the real importance of this journey, the very essence why we are doing this. Once we learned how to forgive, it will give us the strength to overcome whatever challenges might happen next. It will provide us with FREEDOM, and it will be satisfying in the end.

Seek Beneficial Change

We need to seek beneficial change, both emotional and personal. Forgiving someone takes a lot of effort and brings us through the whole journey full of hurt and challenges. Along the way, we'll meet emotions and learn capabilities that we have never encountered before. We'll learn empathy so that the next time someone will cause us wrong, and we can get through it as one. We will understand first before we will react, leading this too much lesser trouble than the other way around to make us mature and more understanding of human beings.

Learn How to be Compassionate Towards Others

As we progress through this journey, we will evolve further as an individual; we will become different from the person we were before, we will understand more of the struggles of other people than we did before. We will learn to put ourselves in their shoes and recognize the reason why they committed a wrongful act.

Compassion towards others is the greatest blessing of this journey. We were acknowledging the fact that the passage of forgiveness is always about the people who hurt us more than ourselves. It is still the very essence of understanding why they did it more than the after-effects to make us a better partner in Marriage.

We need to be able to have the courage to choose to forgive, but then we should keep on choosing it repeatedly. Our spouses are not perfect, flawed sometimes, but then they become a better person over time. So, once they commit a mistake, chose to forgive consistently. In this way, with all the learning involved, we become a better partner in life, and that's what makes it beautiful.

Learn to trust your partner. Yes, they hurt you; they caused you pain—the only way to make it through these steps of forgiveness is to do it together. You are a team. Become one in everything you do. That includes the journey of forgiveness.

Chapter 12: Have a Relationship Game Plan

We have covered a lot of areas that are important to your relationship. The information I have shared with you has helped me through the many years of marriage. They have been tested and proven to work.

One of the biggest things that have helped my relationship is a game plan. I am not talking about a game plan you would have in a basketball game. I am talking about a relationship game plan. I want it to be realistic for you as a couple.

Think about it, have you ever tried to lose weight through one of these companies you pay money too? They create a plan for you to follow so you can lose weight at a safe and healthy rate. It is realistic. They do not promise you will lose 100 pounds by your birthday when your birthday is in seven days. Instead, they promise you will lose 50 pounds if you follow their plan for six months.

Look at your relationship with your spouse. Are you satisfied with your relationship? Most answers are, *"I want to be closer to my spouse."* It does not matter what your relationship is at this moment. It does not matter if you are having issues that hard to solve right now. The thing that you should always remember is never too late to change and make room to make it better.

Your game plan should include these key areas:

- Important Dates
    - Today's date/time/place
    - Follow date/time/place
    - Date of your date night
    - Date of your Family Game Night
    - Any important dates that you do on as a routine with your spouse each week.
- Goals
    - Couple Goals
        - Working on this week
        - Where you want to see your marriage in six months
    - Family Goals
        - Working on this week
        - Where you want to see your relationship in six months
- Areas of Growth
- Support System
- A Mission Statement

Creating a game plan for your relationship will help you stay on track to accomplish your goals and strengthen your marriage. You will see the positivity come into your contact and begin to appreciate your spouse more. You can see

<u>Appendix C</u> for your Relationship Outline Plan and <u>Appendix D</u> for your Marriage Mission Statement page. Use each of these sections to create your game plan and mission statement.

Important Dates

Remembering dates are essential in the relationship, not only doctor's appointments or the company's meeting. I am talking about periods of your weekly family date night. These are dates that you do regularly. They could be weekly or monthly. The point is, they are recurring dates.

Along with these recurring dates, you will also want to include the time you created this game plan, and the date of your next follow up. I recommend that you do a follow up every week. Set a specific time and day that it happens. Always have the follow-ups on the same day and time.

Each follows up is essential to do a check on your relationship goals and ensure you are still on the right track.

Goals

It is essential to have goals. Goals help us to stay focused. In your relationship, you will want to set goals and work to achieve it. These goals can be anything from having a weekly date night to buying a new home. They are one of the building blocks to a great relationship with your spouse. Set goals together. A good and healthy relationship is willing to improve and grow to settle that desired goal.

Do not mix your relationship goals with your wants. That means, do not put on an intention to buy a new house in your relationship game plan. You can create anything game plan that will list those types of goals. Any goal will help you draw closer to each other. However, we will focus on the relationship goals that are the most important for strengthening your marriage.

In the following section, I will talk about areas of growth. Use that section to help guide you to make the right goals. The big question to ask yourself, "where do I want to see our marriage in 6 months, five years, or ten years?"

You should have long-term and short-term goals. Each short-term goal should help you to achieve your long-term goal. Check on your goals during every follow-up to see where you are. Have a checklist on things that still need to do. It will also help you to start in line with your long-term goal.

Areas of Growth

Everyone has areas they need to improve on. Relationships were no different. Use this area to help you identify the areas you can improve in your relationship. What do you not like and your relationship? What would you like to do better?

This section will work for hand in hand with your goals. Focus on the areas of growth and create your goals from your list. Make a list of about 12 cities that you have identified as a couple. Continue to add to this list. When you complete each item on your list and move to the next one, replace those three with new areas of growth. Always have 12 regions at the end of your follow-up.

You will be doing a weekly follow-up; therefore, take three areas you want to focus on create your short-term goals. These will be items you wish to work on throughout the week. Each area you have worked on, continue to do that as you pick the next three cities.

As you move onto three new areas, move to those that you already worked on as a reminder. Just because you worked on them and moved onto the next three does not mean you stop doing it.

Support System

Many couples do not see the need for a support system. It is hard to do it alone. Everyone argues or has problems in their relationship. That is why you need to create a team that will always be there for you and your spouse. Keep in mind, you are a team, and every name on the support system must check upon between both of you.

You can add as many people as you would like. The bigger your team is and the more people you think can help you, the stronger your support system will be. It is time to brainstorm and analyze. Ask these questions:

- ➢ What is important to you that you want in your support team?
- ➢ What can they bring to your relationship?
- ➢ Can you trust them to be there when you need them?

These are only basic questions. You can add to this list to narrow your team down to those who will help strengthen you and not bring you down. Time to start listing everyone you know. As a couple, you will discuss each person. You and your spouse will have a chance to say if they agree or disagree. You should also give your reason for the decision. If you cannot agree, move onto the next person.

Mission Statement

Having a mission statement is a great way to keep your marriage secure. Once created, put it up in our house where you can read it daily. It will serve as a constant daily reminder.   Each time you read it, you will be reminded of why you got married, your goals, your weaknesses, your strengths, and the commitments you have to each other through marriage.

With a constant reminder through a mission statement, it will help you fight temptations and helps you to focus on your goals and to direct you towards a healthy and robust relationship.

What Is Your Fairytale?

It has come to a full circle. In the introduction, I mentioned a fairytale romance. We do not have mermaids turning to humans for love, beautiful princesses sleeping on a bed for a hundred years until they receive a kiss from their true love, or a young lady losing her slipper made of glass because she needed to get home before midnight. These are the fairytales we know and love as a child. Fairytales in the movies and books have "happy ever after" endings. They do not show the struggles and challenges of real life.

Each of us struggles in the relationship. Each of us fights for the things we want, most notably for the person that we love. Everyone has challenges. However, it is about how we handle them and how we act and find a solution. When a couple starts to date, they create memories and experiences. They have their share of hurt, pain, and happiness. These experiences are what creates a deeper connection. These connections make them understand the other person better.

When my wife and I were dating, we went everywhere. That first year, we took over 1,000 pictures. We created memories that will last a lifetime. Even today, we still talk about those experiences after all these years. We still remember those simple details that complete our memories. Our first date was in Seoul, South Korea zoo. We also forgot to eat. The first time I sang to my wife. The zoo was the start of many memories throughout our lives. We have had hard times. We have fought about unimportant things and fights over crazy little things that would not even matter to us. We had disagreements about anything that we don't even know why.

Our greatest achievement happened with the start of our family. This is only the beginning of our story. All our memories created a fairytale of our own. We do not have a *"happy ever after"* relationship that you see in the movies. However, in our eyes, we have a *"happy ever after"* marriage.

Now it is your turn. Start looking at old pictures and flashback those memories. Start remembering how you can not sleep the night before your first date—

looking back to those times that you want to be the real eye-catcher to your spouse's eyes. Recall those times you were dating your spouse before your marriage. What was your first date like? Was it so fun and exciting? What was your reaction when your spouse said their very first *"I love you"*? Was that overwhelming to hear that you find yourself stammering while staring at them? Did your heart collapse inside that you wanted to stop the clock? If the answer is yes, then you have the most beautiful memories to keep in your heart.

Work together to create your own story. Do not leave the hardships, challenges, and temptations out. Those bad things happen in your relationship is part of what you become now as a couple; those hardships and trials were there for a reason. Those challenges arose for us to learn along the way.

They are a part of marriage and being together. There are so many ways to share your story. You can create a scrapbook using your photos, put a little scenario, and write a novel while using your pictures as illustrations or create a digital story through video. The possibilities only limited by your imagination and how you give life to those characters.

What is Your Story?

Use all the techniques I have shared with you to strengthen your marriage. Add those new experiences to your story. Your story will not stop here. It will continue throughout the rest of your lives. We all have a fairytale to tell. What is your fairytale?

Appendix A: Marriage Assessment

Assessing your Marriage is a significant part of your relationship. On each question, I want to think about where your response stands on a scale from 1 – 10. Keep in mind, ten will be *"Yes,"* and one will be *"No."* Take this assessment should take individually. You will compare your scores at the end of the evaluation to get a better understanding of each other.

➢ We look at and approach life in terms of *"us."*

    1   2   3   4   5   6   7   8   9   10

➢ We know how to communicate with a bright and successful understand to finish a project together.

    1   2   3   4   5   6   7   8   9   10

➢ My spouse acknowledges my talents and gifts. They accept me for who I am. They do not try to change who I am.

    1   2   3   4   5   6   7   8   9   10

➢ When I look back on time, we have been together, and I see how I have become a better person and matured.

    1   2   3   4   5   6   7   8   9   10

➢ We have developed a network of friends. These friends provide us with friendship and support.

    1   2   3   4   5   6   7   8   9   10

➢ We have enough money to support the lifestyle we enjoy and are satisfied.

    1   2   3   4   5   6   7   8   9   10

➢ We have agreed and planned for how we spend our money. That includes how much we will pay, how much we will save, how much will be given to charity, etc.

    1   2   3   4   5   6   7   8   9   10

➢ Our relationship has helped me to draw on my inner strength and wisdom, which comes from a spiritual presence.

    1   2   3   4   5   6   7   8   9   10

> We are committed to each other by working on living a healthier me. We are eating a healthy diet, getting plenty of sleep, and getting the exercise our body needs.

      1   2   3   4   5   6   7   8   9   10

> We look at the negatives in life, and we do not have the harmful effects of having too much tobacco, drugs, and alcohol in Marriage.

      1   2   3   4   5   6   7   8   9   10

> I work outside the home, in a home office, or as a homemaker and find my spouse is very supportive of me.

      1   2   3   4   5   6   7   8   9   10

> I have satisfaction with how we share the work around the home.

      1   2   3   4   5   6   7   8   9   10

> We care about what is going on in our community. We enjoy taking the time to reach out to our neighbors and those in need.

      1   2   3   4   5   6   7   8   9   10

> We know what is going on in our community. It is crucial to take part and be active citizens.

      1   2   3   4   5   6   7   8   9   10

> When I am ill, the first person by my side to comfort me will be my spouse, and they are the first person I turn for help.

      1   2   3   4   5   6   7   8   9   10

> When my spouse is ill, I am the first person by their side and the first person they turn to for help.

      1   2   3   4   5   6   7   8   9   10

> My spouse is my partner and best friend. They are the ones I want to spend most of my time with and have fun.

      1   2   3   4   5   6   7   8   9   10

➢ It brings a lot of satisfaction to me when I talk about my feelings and thoughts with my spouse.

    1   2   3   4   5   6   7   8   9   10

➢ My spouse came from a home that welcomed children. They knew how to love and care for them.

    1   2   3   4   5   6   7   8   9   10

➢ I came from a home that welcomed children. My parents knew how to love and care for me.

    1   2   3   4   5   6   7   8   9   10

➢ We have talked about and agreed on the following: (only check the items you have decided on together. One point for each area you check.)

__ How many children you plan on or would like to have.
__ Your methods for planning your family. Include Natural Family Planning.
__ How to balance work with family.
__ How you will share the chores in the house with kids with working, Marriage, and the children.
__ How will you discipline your children.
__ If you can have children.
__ If you are willing to adopt children.
__ Other: _________________________________

➢ Your spouse has proper stress management and knows how to handle the stress.

    1   2   3   4   5   6   7   8   9   10

➢ I have good stress management and know how to handle the stress.

    1   2   3   4   5   6   7   8   9   10

➢ We take great care to know hurt each other with our words or actions during the conflict. We take care of it immediately.

    1   2   3   4   5   6   7   8   9   10

➢ My parents took care of conflicts immediately while ensuring they do not hurt each other with their words or actions.

    1   2   3   4   5   6   7   8   9   10

➢ I am happy and satisfied with the way my spouse expresses their affection. (e.g., kissing, leaving love notes, holding hands, giving hugs, etc.)

    1   2   3   4   5   6   7   8   9   10

➢ Our sexual life is essential, and I am satisfied with how often we make love.

    1   2   3   4   5   6   7   8   9   10

➢ I enjoy or sexual life, and I am satisfied with the enjoyment.

    1   2   3   4   5   6   7   8   9   10

What is your Relationship Status?

You had 28 questions in this assessment. It is time to add up our score and see how you did. _________ **(Total)**

189 or Higher – You are amazing and have a great relationship with your spouse.
135 to 188 – You are doing good. You have a few things to work on; however, you are on the right track to better your relationship.
One hundred thirty-four or less – You are struggling with your relationship. You should take some time to discuss these questions with your spouse and focus on things you can do to strengthen your relationship. The strength or weakness of your bond falls on both of you. You are a team. You can do this.

Healthy Marriage Qualities and Priorities

It is essential to work together as a team. As a team, you should know what the priorities are of the other person. This section will list each of the qualities in Chapter 2: Marriage and Family Assessment and will be focusing on the Marriage Assessment area of the chapter. You will have three choices to help you better understand your priorities.

Teamwork: __My Priority __Spouses Priority __Common Priority
Maturity & Acceptance: __My Priority __Spouses Priority __Common Priority
Community & Faith: __My Priority __Spouses Priority __Common Priority
Wealth Building: __My Priority __Spouses Priority __Common Priority
A Healthy Lifestyle: __My Priority __Spouses Priority __Common Priority
Success in Workplace: __My Priority __Spouses Priority __Common Priority
Being a Good Neighbor: __My Priority __Spouses Priority __Common Priority
Being Friends: __My Priority __Spouses Priority __Common Priority
Welcome Children: __My Priority __Spouses Priority __Common Priority
Emotional/Mental Health: __My Priority __Spouses Priority __Common Priority
Sexual Intimacy/Affection: __My Priority __Spouses Priority __Common Priority

Appendix B: What Is Your Love Language?

Open your mind. Focus hard and concentrate. Do not make the choices based on what you think your spouse wants. Print this page out. You should have one for you and the other for your spouse. Do not look at each other's survey while filling it out.

Directions: The survey divided into five groups. Each group will have five choices. You will rank each option from 1 – 5. 1 will be what you least appreciate, while five will be what you most enjoy. Each sentence will have a number, and each number can only be used one time—answer based on your gender when the question gives you a choice.

Group 1

A: _______ Your spouse tells you, *"You did a great job on that. I appreciate it!"*

B: _______ Your spouse does something unexpected. It could be in or around your room or the house, and you appreciate it.

C: _______ Your spouse stopped at the store and brought you home a surprise treat.

D: _______ Your spouse wants to take a leisure walk and invites you. They want to chat while on the trail.

E: _______ Before your spouse leaves the house, they make a point to embrace you with a hug and kiss.

Group 2

A: _______ Your spouse lets you know how much they appreciate you through words.

B: _______ Your spouse (female) encourages you to take a load off and relax while they wash the car. Your spouse (male) helps you to take charge off and relax while they wash the dishes.

C: _______ Your spouse (female) stops at the store and brings you to home your favorite treat. Your spouse (male) brings you a beautiful bouquet because he loves you.

D: _______ Your spouse asks you to sit with them and asks you about your day.

E: _______ Even if you are passing between rooms, your spouse stops to hug you.

Group 3

A: _______ During a party, your spouse shares with the others about a success you recently had.

B: _______ Your spouse cleans all out the inside of your car.

C: _______ You receive an unexpected gift from your spouse.

D: _______ You receive an unexpected trip from your spouse.
E: _______ Your spouse holds your hand when you are walking through the mall
or when you are at an event, they stand with their arm around your
shoulder.

Group 4

A: _______ Your spouse applauds you for a unique quality you have.
B: _______ You are brought breakfast in bed by your spouse.
C: _______ You are surprised by your spouse with a membership to something
you have been wanting.
D: _______ Your spouse plans a special date night for just the two of you.
E: _______ Your spouse volunteers to take you to an event so you would not
need to ride the bus.

Group 5

A: _______ Your spouse lets you know how much their friends appreciate you.
B: _______ You have an application that needs to fill out, and you have been
dreading it; your spouse, takes the time to fill it out so you would not
need to do it.
C: _______ Your spouse secretly sends you a gift, card, or some other gift in the
mail.
D: _______ Your spouse hijacks you for lunch and surprises you with your favorite
restaurant.
E: _______ You receive a message from your spouse.

You will only need to print this page out once. From your survey, transfer your scores to the score sheet. For example, if you put a 1 in question A for Group 1, you will write a one in the spot. Do this for each answer and all five groups after the responses, transfer to add up the scores. The love language with the highest score will be your primary language, while the next highest will be your secondary language.

The scorecard designed for both of you, re-transfer the result onto the same card, and this allows you to see the differences. On the scorecard, each line is labeled *"H"* for husband and *"W"* for the wife.

The headings are:

> - **WofA:** Words of Affirmation
> - **of:** Acts of Service
> - **G:** Gifts
> - **QT:** Quality Time
> - **PT:** Physical Touch

When completed, refer to Chapter 7: What is your Love Language to see how to better understand the needs of your spouse.

Score Card						
		WofA	WofA	G	QT	PT
Group 1	(H)	A:___	B:___	C:___	D:___	E:___
	(W)	A:___	B:___	C:___	D:___	E:___
Group 2	(H)	A:___	B:___	C:___	D:___	E:___
	(W)	A:___	B:___	C:___	D:___	E:___
Group 3	(H)	A:___	B:___	C:___	D:___	E:___
	(W)	A:___	B:___	C:___	D:___	E:___
Group 4	(H)	A:___	B:___	C:___	D:___	E:___
	(W)	A:___	B:___	C:___	D:___	E:___
Group 5	(H)	A:___	B:___	C:___	D:___	E:___
	(W)	A:___	B:___	C:___	D:___	E:___
Totals	(H)	A:___	B:___	C:___	D:___	E:___
	(W)	A:___	B:___	C:___	D:___	E:___

Now that you have your scores transferred. I want you to write down what your primary and secondary love languages are.

Husband

- ➢ **Primary Love Language:**
- ➢ **Secondary Love Language:**

Wife

- ➢ **Primary Love Language:**
- ➢ **Secondary Love Language:**

Use this new knowledge to learn about your spouse and how they feel the most love and care from you. Stop speaking different languages. It is time to get on the same page, sail together as one and give your partner what they most desire.

Appendix C: Relationship Game Plan

Today's Date: _____________   Follow-Up Date: _____________

Important Dates

Date Night Date: _____________   Family Night Date: _____________
Activity: _____________   Activity: _____________

_____________ Date: _____________   _____________ Date: _____________
Activity: _____________   Activity: _____________

Goals

Long-Term Relationship Goal (Where do I want our relationship to be in 6 months?):

____
____
____

Short-Term Goal 1 (Weekly Area of Growth):

____
____

Short-Term Goal 2 (Weekly Area of Growth):

____
____

Short-Term Goal 3 (Weekly Area of Growth):

____
____

List of Areas of Growth

1: _________   2: _________   3: _________   4: _________
5: _________   6: _________   7: _________   8: _________
9: _________   10: _________   11: _________   12: _________

Worked on Areas of Growth

1: _________   2: _________   3: _________   4: _________
5: _________   6: _________   7: _________   8: _________
9: _________   10: _________   11: _________   12: _________

Appendix D: Your Mission Statement

Having a mission statement is very important for your relationship and your family. I suggest having one for your marriage and a separate one for your family. Make sure the information in each mission statement has similar goals. You do not want them to contradict.

For your mission statement, you will be referring to your game plan that you made as a couple. For each area of the game plan, you will have a different paragraph.

- ➢ Heading
    - o *"Our Marriage Missions Statement"* or
    - o *"Our Family Mission Statement"*
- ➢ 1st Paragraph
    - o List what type of relationship you will have
- ➢ 2nd Paragraph
    - o List your goals
- ➢ 3rd Paragraph
    - o List your weakness
- ➢ 4th Paragraph
    - o List your strengths
- ➢ 5th Paragraph
    - o List how you are going to strengthen your relationship
- ➢ 6th Paragraph
    - o Conclude with your commitment to each other.
- ➢ Bottom
    - o Create a place where you both can sign it.

References & Resources

This is a list of resources for additional information. It also provides a link to the website if there is one available. These are the resources I have used to compile this book and offer you the most significant supply of them all into one book.

Bechtle, M. (27 February 2018). *6 Tools for Healthy Communication in Marriage.* Retrieved from the Focus on the Family website at https://www.focusonthefamily.com/marriage/6-tools-for-healthy-communication-in-marriage/?fbclid=IwAR19DYGcsr2rdRZvagqiGTqCPGabC-nlfTlBn-7DzsqACEl-tYM4jWwoLhY

Craig, H. (4 October 2020). *10 Ways to Build Trust in a Relationship.* Retrieved from PositivePsychology.com at https://positivepsychology.com/build-trust/?fbclid=IwAR0pbRjNy0rQEmsxLN-svAMsx0p8fUj-kfWzDaoGPNsLLJiY1mARAgHUXRU

Everyday Health (17 November 2017). *The 7 Stages of Marriage.* Retrieved from the Everyday Health website at https://www.everydayhealth.com/healthy-living/healthy-home/7-stages-marriage/

Fellizar, K. (16 January 2019). *HOW TO Resist the Temptation to Cheat.* Retrieved from the Bustle website at https://www.bustle.com/p/how-to-resist-the-temptation-to-cheat-15831123?fbclid=IwAR0AAKJDErRDfgS9t93jxmE3IxhJYCer5I4uvhLzxM7DfUjdQVzspOHc7UQ

Gragg, A. (27 March 2019). *12 Dating & Marriage Building Activities.* Retrieved from the Decide Your Legacy website at https://www.decideyourlegacy.com/12-relationship-building-activities/

Gresge, G. (15 September 2016). *4 Ways to Fight Temptation + Use It Actually to Improve Your Relationship.* Retrieved from the BRIT+CO website at https://www.brit.co/how-to-fight-temptation-to-cheat-in-relationship/?fbclid=IwAR07KSe1NeKYaiUJyFgCGqPjEJBh_tvOAa-1z4HjNMAmBRfEjIGJQIkh5MU

Hamilton, L. (20 March 2020). *How Long Does the Honeymoon Phase Last in a Marriage?* Retrieved for the ReGain website at https://www.regain.us/advice/general/how-long-does-the-honeymoon-phase-last-in-a-marriage/

Jones, K. (6 February 2018). *Surviving Marriage After the Honeymoon Period.* Retrieved from marriage.com at https://www.marriage.com/blog/relationship/surviving-marriage-after-the-honeymoon-period/

Perspectives Counseling. (n.d.). *Top 10 At Home Couples Therapy Exercises.* Retrieved from the Perspectives Counseling website at https://perspectivesoftroy.com/couples-therapy-exercises/

Rock Solid Marriages (n.d.). *The Five Stages of Marriage.* Retrieved from the Rock Solid Marriages website at https://www.rocksolidmarriages.com/the-5-stages-of-marriage.html?fbclid=IwAR1B3aJsG08QoCiwYO26mKIS80otYc6uYH3KINjN9mxuyNgdA9I4DYkPlhg

Slattery, J. (8 September 2016). *When You're Attracted to Someone Who's Not Your Spouse.* Retrieved from the Ai website at https://www.authenticintimacy.com/resources/3308/when-youre-attracted-to-someone-whos-not-your-spouse?fbclid=IwAR0YhjyF0Oi2_gxayf86CdjUn26_pMbbAdoS6fS6W_DN2JajdUgWsptpk_s

Smalley, G. (14 July 2017). *Four Types of Communication to Strengthen Your Marriage.* Retrieved from For the Family website at https://www.focusonthefamily.com/marriage/four-types-of-communication-to-strengthen-your-marriage/?fbclid=IwAR1wuNqObcu8YBb1HYz7hfrPX1Iw3cTSDIaTBnIotCExA8mLljc6juTPSlk

Stronger Families. (2011). *Oxygen for Your Relationship.* Retrieved from the Participant Guide.

Timkade. (27 March 2012). *Top 5 Needs of Men and Women.* Retrieved from the Tim Kade blog at https://timkade.wordpress.com/2012/03/27/top-5-needs-of-men-and-women/

Uglow, P. (3 June 2019). *A Heavy Heart: Learning Forgiveness in Marriage.* Retrieved from the Thrive Global website at https://thriveglobal.com/stories/a-heavy-heart-learning-forgiveness-in-marriage/?fbclid=IwAR3fl-4Y07WpFc-TdA5MXaayqdxBGbKclQnzc9ZES3qyvAcGUiRl14xZzfk

Weiss, S. (28 June 2018). *How Long Does the Honeymoon Phase Last? 5 Signs You're Out Of It.* Retrieved from the Bustle website at https://www.bustle.com/p/how-long-does-the-honeymoon-phase-last-5-signs-youre-out-of-it-9204925

Working on Your Marriage. (n.d.). *Marriage Assessment.* Retrieved from the Working on Your Marriage website at http://www.workonyourmarriage.org/marriage-assessment.html

Working on Your Marriage. (n.d.) *Marriage Success Assessment.* Retrieved from the Working on Your Marriage website at http://www.workonyourmarriage.org/support-files/relationship-assessment-2016-12.pdf

About the Author
Barnard W. Bunton

Burton has had his share of heartaches with women. After going through several failed attempts of marriages, he set a goal to learn about what it takes to have a successful marriage of 32 years.

It was after years of studying that Burton found the secret to a successful marriage. Those secrets have helped him raise their two children, along with his wife. His secrets found in the way he writes and the words he says.

Currently, Burton writes about his great discoveries. It brings joy to him to see these secrets helping others to strengthen their marriages. He spends most of his time researching new ways to help others to improve their families and marriages.

Burton says, "The techniques in this book will not only strengthen your marriage but will set an unbreakable bond between you and your spouse." He is passionate about his marriage—the same passion found in his words.

"If you have enjoyed reading this book, I would be very grateful if you could post an honest review. All that you need to do is to click here, then click the blue link next to the yellow stars. On the left, You'll see a gray button that says "Write a customer review"—click that and you're good to go, thank you."

Barnard

www.ingramcontent.com/pod-product-compliance
Lightning Source LLC
Chambersburg PA
CBHW060633080726
47818CB00003B/126